NumPy Essentials

Boost your scientific and analytic capabilities in no time at all by discovering how to build real-world applications with NumPy

Leo (Liang-Huan) Chin

Tanmay Dutta

BIRMINGHAM - MUMBAI

NumPy Essentials

Copyright © 2016 Packt Publishing

First published: April 2016

Production reference: 1220416

Published by Packt Publishing Ltd.
Livery Place
35 Livery Street
Birmingham
B3 2PB, UK.
ISBN 978-1-78439-367-0

www.packtpub.com

Credits

Authors

Leo (Liang-Huan) Chin
Tanmay Dutta

Reviewers

Miklós Prisznyák
Pruthuvi Maheshakya Wijewardena

Commissioning Editor

Kartikey Pandey

Acquisition Editor

Larissa Pinto

Content Development Editor

Rohit Singh

Technical Editor

Murtaza Tinwala

Copy Editor

Sonia Cheema

Project Coordinator

Izzat Contractor

Proofreader

Safis Editing

Indexer

Rekha Nair

Graphics

Kirk D'Penha
Disha Haria
Jason Monteiro

Production Coordinator

Melwyn Dsa

About the Authors

Leo (Liang-Huan) Chin is a data engineer with more than 5 years of experience in the field of Python. He works for Gogoro smart scooter, Taiwan, where his job entails discovering new and interesting biking patterns . His previous work experience includes ESRI, California, USA, which focused on spatial-temporal data mining. He loves data, analytics, and the stories behind data and analytics. He received an MA degree of GIS in geography from State University of New York, Buffalo. When Leo isn't glued to a computer screen, he spends time on photography, traveling, and exploring some awesome restaurants across the world. You can reach Leo at http://chinleock.github.io/portfolio/.

Tanmay Dutta is a seasoned programmer with expertise in programming languages such as Python, Erlang, C++, Haskell, and F#. He has extensive experience in developing numerical libraries and frameworks for investment banking businesses. He was also instrumental in the design and development of a risk framework in Python (pandas, NumPy, and Django) for a wealth fund in Singapore. Tanmay has a master's degree in financial engineering from Nanyang Technological University, Singapore, and a certification in computational finance from Tepper Business School, Carnegie Mellon University.

I would like to thank my wife and my brother for invaluable technical guidance and the rest of my family for supporting and encouraging me to write this book. I would like to express my gratitude to the editors, who provided me with support, encouragement, and valuable comments regarding the content and format and assisted me in the editing of this book. I would like to thank Packt Publishing for giving me the opportunity to coauthor this book.

About the Reviewers

Miklós Prisznyák is a senior software engineer with a scientific background. He graduated as a physicist and worked on his MSc thesis on Monte Carlo simulations of non-Abelian lattice quantum field theories in 1992. Having worked for 3 years at the Central Research Institute for Physics in Hungary, he joined MultiRáció Kft. in Budapest, a company founded by other physicists, which specialized in mathematical data analysis and the forecasting of economic data. It was here that he discovered the Python programming language in 2000. He set up his own consulting company in 2002 and worked on various projects for insurance, pharmacy, and e-commerce companies, using Python whenever he could. He also worked for a European Union research institute in Italy, testing, debugging, and developing a distributed, Python-based Zope/Plone web application. He moved to Great Britain in 2007, and at first, he worked for a Scottish start-up using Twisted Python. He then worked in the aerospace industry in England using, among others, the PyQt windowing toolkit, the Enthought application framework, and the NumPy and SciPy libraries. He returned to Hungary in 2012 and rejoined MultiRáció. Since then, he's mainly worked on a Python extension to OpenOffice/EuroOffice using NumPy and SciPy again, which allows users to solve nonlinear and stochastic optimization problems with the spreadsheet software Calc. He has also used Django, which is the most popular Python web framework currently. Miklós likes to travel and read books, and he is interested in the sciences, mathematics, linguistics, history, politics, go (the board game), and a few other topics. Besides this, he enjoys a good cup of coffee. However, he thinks nothing beats spending time with his brilliant, maths-savvy, Minecraft-programming, 13-year-old son, Zsombor, who also learned English on his own.

Pruthuvi Maheshakya Wijewardena holds a bachelor's degree in engineering from University of Moratuwa, Sri Lanka. He has contributed to the scikit-learn machine learning library as a Google Summer of Code participant and has experience working with the Python language, especially the NumPy, SciPy, pandas, and statsmodels libraries. While studying for his undergraduate degree, he was able to publish his thesis on machine learning. Currently, he works as a software engineer at WSO2, as a part of the data analytics team.

I would like to thank my mother, brothers, teachers, and friends.

For support files and downloads related to your book, please visit www.PacktPub.com.

Did you know that Packt offers eBook versions of every book published, with PDF and ePub files available? You can upgrade to the eBook version at www.PacktPub.com and as a print book customer, you are entitled to a discount on the eBook copy. Get in touch with us at service@packtpub.com for more details.

At www.PacktPub.com, you can also read a collection of free technical articles, sign up for a range of free newsletters and receive exclusive discounts and offers on Packt books and eBooks.

https://www2.packtpub.com/books/subscription/packtlib

Do you need instant solutions to your IT questions? PacktLib is Packt's online digital book library. Here, you can search, access, and read Packt's entire library of books.

Why subscribe?

- Fully searchable across every book published by Packt
- Copy and paste, print, and bookmark content
- On demand and accessible via a web browser

Free access for Packt account holders

If you have an account with Packt at www.PacktPub.com, you can use this to access PacktLib today and view 9 entirely free books. Simply use your login credentials for immediate access.

Table of Contents

Preface

Whether you are new to scientific/analytic programming, or a seasoned expert, this book will provide you with the skills you need to successfully create, optimize, and distribute your Python/NumPy analytical modules.

Starting from the beginning, this book will cover the key features of NumPy arrays and the details of tuning the data format to make it most fit to your analytical needs. You will then get a walkthrough of the core and submodules that are common to various multidimensional, data-typed analysis. Next, you will move on to key technical implementations, such as linear algebra and Fourier analysis. Finally, you will learn about extending your NumPy capabilities for both functionality and performance by using Cython and the NumPy C API. The last chapter of this book also provides advanced materials to help you learn further by yourself.

This guide is an invaluable tutorial if you are planning to use NumPy in analytical projects.

What this book covers

Chapter 1, *An Introduction to NumPy*, is a Getting Started chapter of this book, which provides the instructions to help you set up the environment. It starts with introducing the Scientific Python Module family (SciPy Stack) and explains the key role NumPy plays in scientific computing with Python.

Chapter 2, *The NumPy ndarray Object*, covers the essential usage of NumPy ndarray object, including the initialization, the fundamental attributes, data types, and memory layout. It also covers the theory underneath the operation, which gives you a clear picture of ndarray.

Chapter 3, *Using Numpy Arrays*, is an advanced chapter on NumPy ndarray usage, which continues Chapter 2, The NumPy ndarray Object. It covers the universal functions in NumPy and shows you the tricks to speed up your code. It also shows you the shape manipulation and broadcasting rules.

Chapter 4, *Numpy Core and Libs Submodules*, includes two sections. The first section has detailed explanation about the relationship between the way NumPy ndarray allocates memory and the interaction of CPU cache. The second part of this chapter covers the special NumPy Array containing multiple data types (the structure/record array). Also, this chapter explores the experimental datetime64 module in NumPy.

Chapter 5, *Linear Algebra in NumPy*, starts by utilizing matrix and mathematical computation using linear algebra modules. It shows you multiple ways to solve a mathematical problem: using Matrix, vector decomposition, and polynomials. It also provides concrete practice for curve fitting and regression.

Chapter 6, *Fourier Analysis in NumPy*, covers the signal processing with NumPy FFT module and the Fourier application on amplifying signals/enlarging images without distortion. It also provides the basic usage of the matplotlib package in Python.

Chapter 7, *Building and Distributing NumPy Code*, covers the basic details around packaging and publishing the code in Python. It provides a basic introduction to NumPy-specific setup files and how to build extension modules.

Chapter 8, *Speeding Up NumPy with Cython*, introduces the users to the Cython programming language and introduces readers to techniques that can be used to speed up existing Python code.

Chapter 9, *Introduction to the NumPy C-API*, provides a basic introduction to the NumPy C API and, in general, how to write wrappers around the existing C/C++ library. The chapter aims to provide a gentle introduction along with equipping the readers with a basic knowledge of how to create new wrappers and understand the existing programs.

Chapter 10, *Further Reading*, is the last chapter of this book. It gives a summary of what we've learned in the book and explores 4 SciPy stack Python modules relying on NumPy arrays, which give you ideas about further scientific Python programming.

What you need for this book

For this book, you will need the following setup:

- Python 2.x or 3.x
- NumPy 1.9 (or later)
- IPython Notebook
- Matplotlib 1.3 (or later)
- gnu gcc compiler or equivalent in Windows
- setuptools

Who this book is for

If you know Python, but are new to scientific programming and want to enter the world of scientific computation, or perhaps you are a Python developer with experience in analytics, but want to gain insight to enhance your analytical skills. In either case, NumPy or this book is ideal for you. Learning NumPy and how to apply it to your Python programs is perfect as your next step towards building professional analytical applications. It would be helpful to have a bit of familiarity with basic programming concepts and mathematics, but no prior experience is required. The later chapters cover concepts such as package distribution, speeding-up code, and C/C++ integration, which require a certain amount of programming and debugging know-how. The readers are assumed to be able to build C/C++ programs in their preferred choice of OS (use gcc in linux and cygwin/migw and more in Windows).

Conventions

In this book, you will find a number of text styles that distinguish between different kinds of information. Here are some examples of these styles and an explanation of their meaning.

Code words in text, database table names, folder names, filenames, file extensions, pathnames, dummy URLs, user input, and Twitter handles are shown as follows: "Note that SciPy can mean a number of thing, like the Python module named `scipy`."

A block of code is set as follows:

```
In [42]: print("Hello, World!")
```

Any command-line input or output is written as follows:

```
In [6]: x
Out[6]:
array([[1, 2, 3],
       [2, 3, 4]])
In [7]: x[0,0]
Out[7]: 1
In [8]: x[1,2]
Out[8]: 4
```

New terms and **important words** are shown in bold.

 Warnings or important notes appear in a box like this.

 Tips and tricks appear like this.

Reader feedback

Feedback from our readers is always welcome. Let us know what you think about this book—what you liked or disliked. Reader feedback is important for us as it helps us develop titles that you will really get the most out of.

To send us general feedback, simply e-mail `feedback@packtpub.com`, and mention the book's title in the subject of your message.

If there is a topic that you have expertise in and you are interested in either writing or contributing to a book, see our author guide at `www.packtpub.com/authors`.

Customer support

Now that you are the proud owner of a Packt book, we have a number of things to help you to get the most from your purchase.

Downloading the example code

You can download the example code files for this book from your account at `http://www.packtpub.com`. If you purchased this book elsewhere, you can visit `http://www.packtpub.com/support` and register to have the files e-mailed directly to you.

You can download the code files by following these steps:

1. Log in or register to our website using your e-mail address and password.
2. Hover the mouse pointer on the **SUPPORT** tab at the top.
3. Click on **Code Downloads & Errata**.
4. Enter the name of the book in the **Search** box.

5. Select the book for which you're looking to download the code files.
6. Choose from the drop-down menu where you purchased this book from.
7. Click on **Code Download**.

You can also download the code files by clicking on the **Code Files** button on the book's webpage at the Packt Publishing website. This page can be accessed by entering the book's name in the **Search** box. Please note that you need to be logged in to your Packt account.

Once the file is downloaded, please make sure that you unzip or extract the folder using the latest version of:

- WinRAR / 7-Zip for Windows
- Zipeg / iZip / UnRarX for Mac
- 7-Zip / PeaZip for Linux

Downloading the color images of this book

We also provide you with a PDF file that has color images of the screenshots/diagrams used in this book. The color images will help you better understand the changes in the output. You can download this file from `https://www.packtpub.com/sites/default/files/downloads/NumPyEssentials_ColoredImages.pdf`.

Errata

Although we have taken every care to ensure the accuracy of our content, mistakes do happen. If you find a mistake in one of our books—maybe a mistake in the text or the code—we would be grateful if you could report this to us. By doing so, you can save other readers from frustration and help us improve subsequent versions of this book. If you find any errata, please report them by visiting `http://www.packtpub.com/submit-errata`, selecting your book, clicking on the **Errata Submission Form** link, and entering the details of your errata. Once your errata are verified, your submission will be accepted and the errata will be uploaded to our website or added to any list of existing errata under the Errata section of that title.

To view the previously submitted errata, go to `https://www.packtpub.com/books/content/support` and enter the name of the book in the search field. The required information will appear under the **Errata** section.

Piracy

Piracy of copyrighted material on the Internet is an ongoing problem across all media. At Packt, we take the protection of our copyright and licenses very seriously. If you come across any illegal copies of our works in any form on the Internet, please provide us with the location address or website name immediately so that we can pursue a remedy.

Please contact us at copyright@packtpub.com with a link to the suspected pirated material.

We appreciate your help in protecting our authors and our ability to bring you valuable content.

Questions

If you have a problem with any aspect of this book, you can contact us at questions@packtpub.com, and we will do our best to address the problem.

1
An Introduction to NumPy

"I'd rather do math in a general-purpose language than try to do general-purpose programming in a math language."

- John D Cook

Python has become one of the most popular programming languages in scientific computing over the last decade. The reasons for its success are numerous, and these will gradually become apparent as you proceed with this book. Unlike many other mathematical languages, such as MATLAB, R and Mathematica, Python is a general-purpose programming language. As such, it provides a suitable framework to build scientific applications and extend them further into any commercial or academic domain. For example, consider a (somewhat) simple application that requires you to write a piece of software and predicts the popularity of a blog post. Usually, these would be the steps that you'd take to do this:

1. Generating a corpus of blog posts and their corresponding ratings (assuming that the ratings here are suitably quantifiable).
2. Formulating a model that generates ratings based on content and other data associated with the blog post.
3. Training a model on the basis of the data you found in step 1. Keep doing this until you are confident of the reliability of the model.
4. Deploying the model as a web service.

Normally, as you move through these steps, you will find yourself jumping between different software stacks. Step 1 requires a lot of web scraping. Web scraping is a very common problem, and there are tools in almost every programming language to scrape the Web (if you are already using Python, you would probably choose Beautiful Soup or Scrapy). Steps 2 and 3 involve solving a machine learning problem and require the use of sophisticated mathematical languages or frameworks, such as Weka or MATLAB, which are only a few of the vast variety of tools that provide machine learning functionality. Similarly, step 4 can be implemented in many ways using many different tools. There isn't one right answer. Since this is a problem that has been amply studied and solved (to a reasonable extent) by a lot of scientists and software developers, getting a working solution would not be difficult. However, there are issues, such as stability and scalability, that might severely restrict your choice of programming languages, web frameworks, or machine learning algorithms in each step of the problem. This is where Python wins over most other programming languages. All the preceding steps (and more) can be accomplished with only Python and a few third-party Python libraries. This flexibility and ease of developing software in Python is precisely what makes it a comfortable host for a scientific computing ecosystem. A very interesting interpretation of Python's prowess as a mature application development language can be found in *Python Data Analysis, Ivan Idris, Packt Publishing*. Precisely, Python is a language that is used for rapid prototyping, and it is also used to build production-quality software because of the vast scientific ecosystem it has acquired over time. The cornerstone of this ecosystem is NumPy.

Numerical Python (**NumPy**) is a successor to the Numeric package. It was originally written by Travis Oliphant to be the foundation of a scientific computing environment in Python. It branched off from the much wider SciPy module in early 2005 and had its first stable release in mid-2006. Since then, it has enjoyed growing popularity among Pythonists who work in the mathematics, science, and engineering fields. The goal of this book is to make you conversant enough with NumPy so that you're able to use it and can build complex scientific applications with it.

The scientific Python stack

Let's begin by taking a brief tour of the **Scientific Python (SciPy)** stack.

Note that SciPy can mean a number of things: the Python module named scipy (http://www.scipy.org/scipylib), the entire SciPy stack (http://www.scipy.org/about.html), or any of the three conferences on scientific Python that take place all over the world.

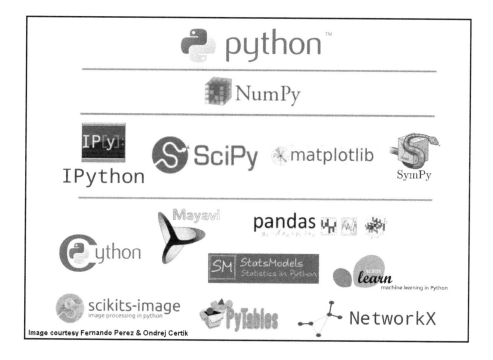

Figure 1: The SciPy stack, standard, and extended libraries

Fernando Perez, the primary author of IPython, said in his keynote at PyCon, Canada 2012:

"Computing in science has evolved not only because software has evolved, but also because we, as scientists, are doing much more than just floating point arithmetic."

This is precisely why the SciPy stack boasts such rich functionality. The evolution of most of the SciPy stack is motivated by teams of scientists and engineers trying to solve scientific and engineering problems in a general-purpose programming language. A one-line explanation of why NumPy matters so much is that it provides the core multidimensional array object that is necessary for most tasks in scientific computing. This is why it is at the root of the SciPy stack. NumPy provides an easy way to interface with legacy Fortran and C/C++ numerical code using time-tested scientific libraries, which we know have been working well for decades. Companies and labs across the world use Python to glue together legacy code that has been around for a long time. In short, this means that NumPy allows us to stand on the shoulders of giants; we do not have to reinvent the wheel. It is a dependency for every other SciPy package. The NumPy ndarray object, which is the subject of the next chapter, is essentially a Pythonic interface to data structures used by libraries written in Fortran, C, and, C++. In fact, the internal memory layouts used by NumPy ndarray objects implement C and Fortran layouts. This will be addressed in detail in upcoming chapters.

The next layer in the stack consists of SciPy, matplotlib, IPython (the interactive shell of Python; we will use it for the examples throughout the book, and details of its installation and usage will be provided in later sections), and SymPy modules. SciPy provides the bulk of the scientific and numerical functionality that a major part of the ecosystem relies on. Matplotlib is the de facto plotting and data visualization library in Python. IPython is an increasingly popular interactive environment for scientific computing in Python. In fact, the project has had such active development and enjoyed such popularity that it is no longer limited to Python and extends its features to other scientific languages, particularly R and Julia. This layer in the stack can be thought of as a bridge between the core array-oriented functionality of NumPy and the domain-specific abstractions provided by the higher layers of the stack. These domain-specific tools are commonly called SciKits-popular ones among them are scikit-image (image processing), scikit-learn (machine learning), statsmodels (statistics), pandas (advanced data analysis), and so on. Listing every scientific package in Python would be nearly impossible since the scientific Python community is very active, and there is always a lot of development happening for a large number of scientific problems. The best way to keep track of projects is to get involved in the community. It is immensely useful to join mailing lists, contribute to code, use the software for your daily computational needs, and report bugs. One of the goals of this book is to get you interested enough to actively involve yourself in the scientific Python community.

The need for NumPy arrays

A fundamental question that beginners ask is. Why are arrays necessary for scientific computing at all? Surely, one can perform complex mathematical operations on any abstract data type, such as a list. The answer lies in the numerous properties of arrays that make them significantly more useful. In this section, let's go over a few of these properties to emphasize why something such as the NumPy `ndarray` object exists at all.

Representing of matrices and vectors

The abstract mathematical concepts of matrices and vectors are central to many scientific problems. Arrays provide a direct semantic link to these concepts. Indeed, whenever a piece of mathematical literature makes reference to a matrix, one can safely think of an array as the software abstraction that represents the matrix. In scientific literature, an expression such as A_{ij} is typically used to denote the element in the ith row and j^{th} column of array A. The corresponding expression in NumPy would simply be *A[i,j]*. For matrix operations, NumPy arrays also support vectorization (details are addressed in Chapter 3, *Using NumPy Arrays*), which speeds up execution greatly. Vectorization makes the code more concise, easier to read, and much more akin to mathematical notation. Like matrices, arrays can be multidimensional too. Every element of an array is addressable through a set of integers called **indices**, and the process of accessing elements of an array with sets of integers is called **indexing**. This functionality can indeed be implemented without using arrays, but this would be cumbersome and quite unnecessary.

Efficiency

Efficiency can mean a number of things in software. The term may be used to refer to the speed of execution of a program, its data retrieval and storage performance, its memory overhead (the memory consumed when a program is executing), or its overall throughput. NumPy arrays are better than most other data structures with respect to almost all of these characteristics (with a few exceptions such as pandas, DataFrames, or SciPy's sparse matrices, which we shall deal with in later chapters). Since NumPy arrays are statically typed and homogenous, fast mathematical operations can be implemented in compiled languages (the default implementation uses C and Fortran). Efficiency (the availability of fast algorithms working on homogeneous arrays) makes NumPy popular and important.

Ease of development

The NumPy module is a powerhouse of off-the-shelf functionality for mathematical tasks. It adds greatly to Python's ease of development. The following is a brief summary of what the module contains, most of which we shall explore in this book. A far more detailed treatment of the NumPy module is in the definitive *Guide to NumPy, Travis Oliphat*. The NumPy API is so flexible that it has been adopted extensively by the scientific Python community as the standard API to build scientific applications. Examples of how this standard is applied across scientific disciplines can be found in *The NumPy Array: a structure for efficient numerical computation, Van Der Walt*, and others:

Submodule	Contents
numpy.core	Basic objects
lib	Additional utilities
linalg	Basic linear algebra
fft	Discrete Fourier transforms
random	Random number generators
distutils	Enhanced build and distribution
testing	Unit testing
f2py	Automatic wrapping of the Fortran code

NumPy in Academia and Industry

It is said that, if you stand at Times Square long enough, you will meet everyone in the world. By now, you must have been convinced that NumPy is the Times Square of SciPy. If you are writing scientific applications in Python, there is not much you can do without digging into NumPy. Figure 2 shows the scope of SciPy in scientific computing at varying levels of abstraction. The red arrow denotes the various low-level functions that are expected of scientific software, and the blue arrow denotes the different application domains that exploit these functions. Python, armed with the SciPy stack, is at the forefront of the languages that provide these capabilities.

A Google Scholar search for NumPy returns nearly 6,280 results. Some of these are papers and articles about NumPy and the SciPy stack itself, and many more are about NumPy's applications in a wide variety of research problems. Academics love Python, which is showcased by the increasing popularity of the SciPy stack as the primary language of scientific programming in countless universities and research labs all over the world. The experiences of many scientists and software professionals have been published on the Python website:

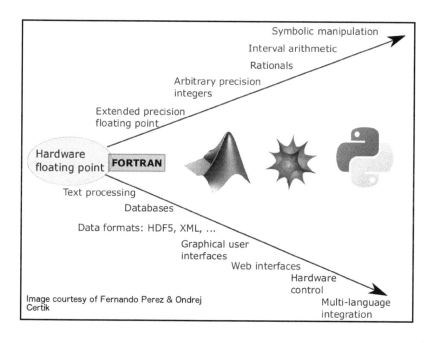

Figure 2: Python versus other languages

Code conventions used in the book

Now that the credibility of Python and NumPy has been established, let's get our hands dirty.

The default environment used for all Python code in this book will be IPython. Instructions on how to install IPython and other tools follow in the next section. Throughout the book, you will only have to enter input in either the command window or the IPython prompt. Unless otherwise specified, `code` will refer to Python code, and `command` will refer to bash or DOS commands.

All Python input code will be formatted in snippets like these:

```
In [42]: print("Hello, World!")
```

`In [42]:` in the preceding snippet indicates that this is the 42nd input to the IPython session. Similarly, all input to the command line will be formatted as follows:

```
$ python hello_world.py
```

On Windows systems, the same command will look something like this:

```
C:\Users\JohnDoe> python hello_world.py
```

For the sake of consistency, the $ sign will be used to denote the command-line prompt, regardless of OS. Prompts, such as `C:\Users\JohnDoe>`, will not appear in the book. While, conventionally, the $ sign indicates bash prompts on Unix systems, the same commands (without typing the actual dollar sign or any other character), can be used on Windows too. If, however, you are using Cygwin or Git Bash, you should be able to use Bash commands on Windows too.

Note that Git Bash is available by default if you install Git on Windows.

Installation requirements

Let's take a look at the various requirements we need to set up before we proceed.

Using Python distributions

The three most important Python modules you need for this book are NumPy, IPython, and matplotlib; in this book, the code is based on the Python 3.4/2.7- compatible version, NumPy version 1.9, and matplotlib 1.4.3. The easiest way to install these requirements (and more) is to install a complete Python distribution, such as Enthought Canopy, EPD, Anaconda, or Python (x,y). Once you have installed any one of these, you can safely skip the remainder of this section and should be ready to begin.

Note for Canopy users: You can use the Canopy GUI, which includes an embedded IPython console, a text editor, and IPython notebook editors. When working with the command line, for best results use the **Canopy Terminal** found in Canopy's Tools menu.

Note for Windows OS users: Besides the Python distribution, you can also install the prebuilt Windows python extended packages from Ghristoph Gohlke's website at `http://www.lfd.uci.edu/~gohlke/pythonlibs/`

Using Python package managers

You can also use Python package managers, such enpkg, Conda, pip or easy_install, to install the requirements using one of the following commands; replace `numpy` with any other package name you'd like to install, for example, `ipython`, `matplotlib` and so on:

```
$ pip install numpy
$ easy_install numpy
$ enpkg numpy # for Canopy users
$ conda install numpy # for Anaconda users
```

Using native package managers

If the Python interpreter you want to use comes with the OS and is not a third-party installation, you may prefer using OS-specific package managers such as aptitude, yum, or Homebrew. The following table illustrates the package managers and the respective commands used to install NumPy:

Package managers	Commands
Aptitude	`$ sudo apt-get install python-numpy`
Yum	`$ yum install python-numpy`
Homebrew	`$ brew install numpy`

Note that, when installing NumPy (or any other Python modules) on OS X systems with Homebrew, Python should have been originally installed with Homebrew.

Detailed installation instructions are available on the respective websites of NumPy, IPython, and matplotlib. As a precaution, to check whether NumPy was installed properly, open an IPython terminal and type the following commands:

```
In [1]: import numpy as np
In [2]: np.test()
```

If the first statement looks like it does nothing, this is a good sign. If it executes without any output, this means that NumPy was installed and has been imported properly into your Python session. The second statement runs the NumPy test suite. It is not critically necessary, but one can never be too cautious. Ideally, it should run for a few minutes and produce the test results. It may generate a few warnings, but these are no cause for alarm. If you wish, you may run the test suites of IPython and matplotlib, too.

 Note that the matplotlib test suite only runs reliably if matplotlib has been installed from a source. However, testing matplotlib is not very necessary. If you can import matplotlib without any errors, it indicates that it is ready for use.

Congratulations! We are now ready to begin.

Summary

In this chapter, we introduced ourselves to the NumPy module. We took a look at how NumPy is a useful software tool to have for those of you who are working in scientific computing. We installed the software required to proceed through the rest of this book.

In next chapter, we will get to the powerful NumPy `ndarray` object, showing you how to use it efficiently.

2
The NumPy ndarray Object

Array-oriented computing is the very heart of computational sciences. It is something that most Python programmers are not accustomed to. Though list or dictionary comprehension is relative to an array and sometimes used similarly to an array, there is a huge difference between a list/dictionary and an array in terms of performance and manipulation. This chapter introduces a basic array object in NumPy. It covers the information that can be gleaned from the intrinsic characteristics of NumPy arrays without performing any external operations on the array.

The topics that will be covered in the chapter are as follows:

- **numpy.ndarray** and how to use it-basic array-oriented computing
- Performance of numpy.ndarray-memory access, storage, and retrieval
- Indexing, slicing, views, and copies
- Array data types

Getting started with numpy.ndarray

In this section, we will go over some of the internals of numpy ndarray, including its structure and behavior. Let's start. Type in the following statements in the IPython prompt:

```
In [1]: import numpy as np

In [2]: x = np.array([[1,2,3],[2,3,4]])

In [3]: print(x)
```

[handwritten: main point here seems to be, always use `import numpy as np`]

NumPy shares the names of its functions with functions in other modules, such as the math module in the Python standard library. Using imports like the following there is not recommended:

```
from numpy import *
```

As it may overwrite many functions that are already in the global namespace, which is not recommended. This may lead to unexpected behavior from your code and may introduce very subtle bugs in it . This may also create conflicts in the code itself, (example numPy has any and will cause conflicts with the system any keyword) and may cause confusion when reviewing or debugging a piece of code. Therefore, it is important and recommended to always follow the import numPy with explicit name such as np convention used in the first line: , — import numpy as np, which is the standard convention used for the purpose of for importing, as it helps the a developer figure out where a function comes from. This can prevent a lot of confusion in large programs..

NumPy arrays can be created in a number of ways, as we shall see. One of the simplest ways of creating arrays is using the array function. Notice that we passed a list of lists to the function, and the constituent lists were equal in length. Each constituent list became a row in the array, and the elements of these lists populated the columns of the resulting array. The array function can be called on lists or even nested lists. Since the level of nesting in our input here was two, the resulting array is two-dimensional. This means that the array can be indexed with a set of two integers. The simplest way of calculating the dimensionality of an array is by checking the ndim attribute of the array:

```
In [4]: x.ndim

Out [4]: 2
```

This can also be accomplished in a different (and indirect) way-by checking the shape attribute of the array. The dimensionality of the array will be equal to how many numbers you see in the shape attribute. (Note that this, however, is not the purpose of the shape attribute.):

```
In [5]: x.shape

Out [5]: (2, 3)
```

This means that the array has two rows and three columns. It is important to note that, unlike MATLAB and R, the indexing of NumPy arrays is zero-based; that is, the first element of a NumPy array is indexed by a zero and the last element is indexed by the integer n-1, where n is the length of the array along the respective dimension. Thus, in the case of the array we just created, the element in the top-left corner of the array can be accessed using a pair of zeros, and the one in the bottom-right corner can be accessed with indices (1,2):

```
In [6]: x

Out[6]:
array([[1, 2, 3],
       [2, 3, 4]])

In [7]: x[0,0]

Out[7]: 1

In [8]: x[1,2]

Out[8]: 4
```

probably need a . after the x

The ndarray object has a lot of useful methods. To get a list of the methods that can be called on an ndarray object, type the `array` variable (in the preceding example, it's x) in the IPython prompt and press Tab. This should list all the methods available for the object. As an exercise, try playing around with a few of them.

Array indexing and slicing

NumPy provides powerful indexing capabilities for arrays. Indexing capabilities in NumPy became so popular that many of them were added back to Python.

Indexing NumPy arrays, in many ways, is very similar to indexing lists or tuples. There are some differences, which will become apparent as we proceed. To start with, let's create an array that has 100 x 100 dimensions:

```
In [9]: x = np.random.random((100, 100))
```

when need () when using a method, and when don't need ()?
could it be that need () when the method applies to/makes use of the elements in the object, and don't need then

when the method applies to the object itself?

Simple integer indexing works by typing indices within a pair of square brackets and placing this next to the array variable. This is a widely used Python construct. Any object that has a __getitem__ method will respond to such indexing. Thus, to access the element in the 42nd row and 87th column, just type this:

```
In [10]: y = x[42, 87]
```

Like lists and other Python sequences, the use of a colon to index a range of values is also supported. The following statement will print the kth row of the x matrix.

```
In [11]: print(x[k, :])
```

The colon can be thought of as an *all elements* character. So, the preceding statement actually means Print all the characters for the kth row. Similarly, a column can be accessed with x[:, k]. Reversing an array is also similar to reversing a list, such as x[::-1].

The indexed portion of an array is also called a *slice* of an array, which creates a copy of a port or the whole array (we will cover copies and views in a later section). In the context of an array, the words "slicing" and "indexing" can generally be used interchangeably.

A very concise overview of different slicing and indexing techniques is shown in the following image:

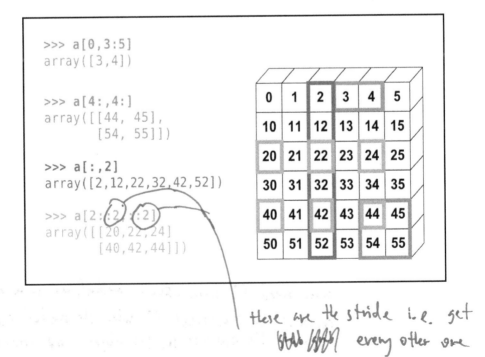

These are the stride i.e. get every other one

Memory layout of ndarray

A particularly interesting attribute of the ndarray object is `flags`. Type the following code:

```
In [12]: x.flags
```

It should produce something like this:

```
Out[12]:
   C_CONTIGUOUS : True
   F_CONTIGUOUS : False
   OWNDATA : True
   WRITEABLE : True
   ALIGNED : True
   UPDATEIFCOPY : False
```

The `flags` attribute holds information about the memory layout of the array. The `C_CONTIGUOUS` field in the output indicates whether the array was a C-style array. This means that the indexing of this array is done like a C array. This is also called row-major indexing in the case of 2D arrays. This means that, when moving through the array, the row index is incremented first, and then the column index is incremented. In the case of a multidimensional C-style array, the last dimension is incremented first, followed by the last but one, and so on.

Similarly, the `F_CONTIGUOUS` attribute indicates whether the array is a Fortran-style array. Such an array is said to have column-major indexing (R, Julia, and MATLAB use column-major arrays). This means that, when moving through the array, the first index (along the column) is incremented first.

Knowing the difference between indexing styles is important, especially for large arrays, because operations on arrays can be significantly sped up if the indexing is applied in the right way. Let's demonstrate this with an exercise.

Declare an array, as follows:

```
In [13]: c_array = np.random.rand(10000, 10000)
```

This will produce a variable called `c_array`, which is a 2D array with a hundred million random numbers as its elements. (We used the `rand` function from the `random` submodule in NumPy, which we will deal with in a later section). Next, create a Fortran–styled array from `c_array`, as follows:

```
In [14]: f_array = np.asfortranarray(c_array)
```

You can check whether `c_array` and `f_array` are indeed C and Fortran-styled, respectively, by reading their `flags` attributes. Next, we define the following two functions:

```
In [15]: def sum_row(x):
             '''
             Given an array `x`, return the sum of its zeroth row.
             '''
             return np.sum(x[0, :])
In [16]: def sum_col(x):
             '''
             Given an array `x`, return the sum of its zeroth column.
             '''
             return np.sum(x[:, 0])
```

Now, let's test the performance of the two functions on both the arrays using IPython's `%timeit` magic function:

There are a handful of magic functions that IPython provides to help us understand the code better; for further details, refer to: `http://ipython. readthedocs.org/en/stable/interactive/magics.html?highlig ht=magic`.

```
In [17]: %timeit sum_row(c_array)
10000 loops, best of 3: 21.2 µs per loop

In [18]: %timeit sum_row(f_array)
10000 loops, best of 3: 157 µs per loop

In [19]: %timeit sum_col(c_array)
10000 loops, best of 3: 162 µs per loop

In [20]: %timeit sum_col(f_array)
10000 loops, best of 3: 21.4 µs per loop
```

As we can see, summing up the row of a C array is much faster than summing up its column. This is because, in a C array, elements in a row are laid out in successive memory locations. The opposite is true for a Fortran array, where the elements of a column are laid out in consecutive memory locations.

 Note that the exact figures may vary depending on the operating system, RAM, and the Python distribution being used, but the relative order between the execution times should remain the same.

This is an important distinction and allows you to suitably arrange your data in an array, depending on the kind of algorithm or operation you are performing. Knowing this distinction can help you speed up your code by orders of magnitude.

Views and copies

There are primarily two ways of accessing data by slicing and indexing. They are called copies and views: you can either access elements directly from an array, or create a copy of the array that contains only the accessed elements. Since a view is a reference of the original array (in Python, all variables are references), modifying a view modifies the original array too. This is not true for copies.

The `may_share_memory` function in NumPy miscellaneous routines can be used to determine whether two arrays are copies or views of each other. While this method does the job in most cases, it is not always reliable, since it uses heuristics. It may return incorrect results too. For introductory purposes, however, we shall take it for granted.

Generally, slicing an array creates a view and indexing it creates a copy. Let us study these differences through a few code snippets. First, let's create a random *100×10* array.

```
In [21]: x = np.random.rand(100,10)
```

Now, let us extract the first five rows of the array and assign them to variable `y`.

```
In [22]: y = x[:5, :]
```

Let us see if `y` is a view of `x`.

```
In [23]: np.may_share_memory(x, y)
```

slice, so according to above it creates a view

```
Out[23]: True
```

Now let us modify the array y and see how it affects x. Set all the elements of y to zero:

```
In [24]: y[:] = 0
```

modifying a view modifies the original array

```
In [25]: print(x[:5, :])
Out[25]: [[ 0.  0.  0.  0.  0.  0.  0.  0.  0.  0.]
 [ 0.  0.  0.  0.  0.  0.  0.  0.  0.  0.]
 [ 0.  0.  0.  0.  0.  0.  0.  0.  0.  0.]
 [ 0.  0.  0.  0.  0.  0.  0.  0.  0.  0.]
 [ 0.  0.  0.  0.  0.  0.  0.  0.  0.  0.]]
```

or thought of another way - the data in y is a subset of the data in x but it's the same data

The code snippet prints out five rows of zeros. This is because y was just a view, a reference to x.

Next, let's create a copy to see the difference. We use the preceding method that uses a random function to create the x array, but this time we initialize the y array using numpy.empty to create an empty array first and then copy the values from x to y. So, now y is not a view/reference of x anymore; it's an independent array but has the same values as part of x. Let's use the may_share_memory function again to verify that y is the copy of x:

```
In [26]: x = np.random.rand(100,10)

In [27]: y = np.empty([5, 10])

In [28]: y[:] = x[:5, :]

In [29]: np.may_share_memory(x, y)
Out[29]: False
```

Let's alter the value in y and check whether the value of x changes as well:

```
In [30]: y[:] = 0
In [31]: print(x[:5, :])
```

You should see the preceding snippet print out five rows of random numbers as we initialized x, so changing y to didn't affect x.

Creating arrays

Arrays can be created in a number of ways, for instance from other data structures, by reading files on disk, or from the Web. For the purposes of this chapter, whose aim is to familiarize us with the core characteristics of a NumPy array, we will be creating arrays using lists or various NumPy functions.

Creating arrays from lists

The simplest way to create an array is using the `array` function. To create a valid array object, arguments to array functions need to adhere to at least one of the following conditions:

- It has to be a valid iterable value or sequence, which may be nested
- It must have an __array__ method that returns a valid numpy array

Consider the following snippet:

```
In [32]: x = np.array([1, 2, 3])

In [33]: y = np.array(['hello', 'world'])
```

The first condition is always true for Python lists and tuples. When creating an array from lists or tuples, the input may consist of different (heterogeneous) data types. The array function, however, will normally cast all input elements into the most suitable data type required for the array. For example, if a list contains both floats and integers, the resulting array will be of type float. If it contains an integer and a boolean, the resulting array will consist of integers. As an exercise, try creating arrays from lists that contain arbitrary data types.

One of the most handy ways of creating lists, and therefore arrays, of integers is using the `range` function:

```
In [34]: x = range(5)

In [35]: y = np.array(x)
```

NumPy has a convenient function, called `arange`, that combines the functionality of the `range` and `array` functions. The preceding two lines of code are equivalent to this:

```
In [36]: x = np.arange(5)
```

For multidimensional arrays, the input lists simply have to be nested, as follows:

```
In [37]: x = np.array([[1, 2, 3],[4, 5, 6]])

In [38]: x.ndim
Out[38]: 2

In [39]: x.shape
Out[39]: (2, 3)
```

The preceding examples simply show how to create a NumPy array from an existing array or from a range of numbers. Next, we will talk about creating an array with random numbers.

Creating random arrays

The `random` module in NumPy provides various functions to create random arrays of any data type. We will be using this module very frequently throughout the book to demonstrate the working of functions in NumPy. The `random` module broadly consists of functions that:

- Create random arrays
- Create random permutations of arrays
- Generate arrays with specific probability distributions

We shall go over each of these in detail through out the book. For the purposes of this chapter, we will be focusing on two important functions in the `random` module-rand and random. Here is a simple snippet demonstrating the use of both these functions:

```
In [40]: x = np.random.rand(2, 2, 2)

In [41]: print(x.shape)
Out[41]: (2, 2, 2)

In [42]: shape_tuple = (2, 3, 4)

In [43]: y = np.random.random(shape_tuple)

In [44]: print(y.shape)
Out[44]: (2, 3, 4)
```

(handwritten annotations: integers; tuple; could use integers if they are put into a tuple i.e. need (( )))

Notice the subtle difference between the arguments passed to the two functions. The random function accepts a *tuple* as an argument and creates an array with dimensionality equal to the length of the tuple. The respective dimensions have their lengths equal to the elements of the tuple. The rand function, on the other hand, takes any number of *integer arguments* and returns a random array such that its dimensionality is equal to the number of integer arguments passed to the function, and the respective dimensions have lengths equal to the values of the integer arguments. Thus, x in the preceding snippet is a three-dimensional array (the number of the arguments passed to the function), and each of the three dimensions of x has a length of 2 (the value of each of the arguments). rand is a convenience function for random. Both these functions can be used interchangeably, provided the arguments that are passed are respectively valid for either function.

These two functions, however, have a major drawback-they can only create arrays of floats. If we wanted an array of random integers, we would have to cast the output of these functions into integers. But this, too, is a significant problem, since NumPy's int function truncates a float to the nearest integer toward zero (this is an equivalent of the floor function). Therefore, casting the output of rand or random to integers will always return an array of zeros since both these functions return floats within the interval (,1). The problem can be solved using the randint function, as follows:

```
In [45]: LOW, HIGH = 1, 11

In [46]: SIZE = 10

In [47]: x = np.random.randint(LOW, HIGH, size=SIZE)

In [48]: print(x)
Out[48]: [ 6  9 10  7  9  5  8  8  9  3]
```

The randint function takes three arguments, of which two are optional. The first argument denotes the desired lower limit of the output values, and the second optional argument denotes the (exclusive) upper limit of the output values. The optional size argument is a tuple that determines the shape of the output array.

There are many other functions, such as seeding the random number generator in the random submodule. For details, refer to:

http://docs.scipy.org/doc/numpy/reference/routines.random.html

Other arrays

There are a few other array creation functions, such as `zeros()`, `ones()`, `eye()`, and others (similar to the ones in MATLAB) that can be used to create NumPy arrays. Their use is fairly straightforward. Arrays can also be populated from files or from the Web. We shall deal with file I/O in the next chapter.

Array data types

Data types are another important intrinsic aspect of a NumPy array alongside its memory layout and indexing. The data type of a NumPy array can be found by simply checking the `dtype` attribute of the array. Try out the following examples to check the data types of different arrays:

```
In [49]: x = np.random.random((10,10))

In [50]: x.dtype
Out[50]: dtype('float64')
In [51]: x = np.array(range(10))

In [52]: x.dtype
Out[52]: dtype('int32')

In [53]: x = np.array(['hello', 'world'])

In [54]: x.dtype
Out [54]: dtype('S5')
```
my system shows dtype('<U7')

Many array creation functions provide a default array data type. For example, the `np.zeros` and `np.ones` functions create arrays that are full of floats by default. But it is possible to make them create arrays of other data types too. Consider the following examples that demonstrate how to use the dtype argument to create arrays of arbitrary data types.

```
In [55]: x = np.ones((10, 10), dtype=np.int)

In [56]: x.dtype
Out[56]: dtype('int32')

In [57]: x = np.zeros((10, 10), dtype='|S1')

In [58]: x.dtype
Out[58]: dtype('S1')
```
not sure why need this, but apparently do need it or M a <

For a complete list of data types supported by NumPy, refer to `http://docs.scipy.org/doc/numpy/user/basics.types.html`.

Summary

In this chapter, we covered some basics of the NumPy ndarray object. We studied some elementary ways of creating NumPy arrays. We also took a look at the differences between copies and views of arrays and how these can affect using indexing and slicing. We saw the subtle differences between the memory layouts offered by NumPy. We are now equipped with the basic vocabulary of the ndarray object and can get started on the core functionality of NumPy. In the next chapter, we will explore more details of ndarray and show you some of them using certain tricks and tips (universal functions and shape manipulation) to make your NumPy script speed up!

3
Using NumPy Arrays

The beauty of NumPy Arrays is that you can use array indexing and slicing to quickly access your data or perform a computation while keeping the efficiency as the C arrays. There are also plenty of mathematical operations that are supported. In this chapter, we will take an in-depth look at using NumPy Arrays. After this chapter, you will feel comfortable using NumPy Arrays and the bulk of their functionality.

Here is a list of topics that will be covered in this chapter:

- Basic operations and the attributes of NumPy Arrays
- Universal functions (ufuncs) and helper functions
- Broadcasting rules and shape manipulation
- Masking NumPy Arrays

"vectorized" means "no looping"

Vectorized operations

All NumPy operations are vectorized, where you apply operations to the whole array instead of on each element individually. This is not just neat and handy but also improves the performance of computation compared to using loops. In this section, we will experience the power of NumPy vectorized operations. A key idea worth keeping in mind before we start exploring this subject is to always think of entire sets of arrays instead of each element; this will help you enjoy learning about NumPy Arrays and their performance. Let's start by doing some simple calculations with scalars and between NumPy Arrays:

```
In [1]: import numpy as np
In [2]: x = np.array([1, 2, 3, 4])
In [3]: x + 1
Out[3]: array([2, 3, 4, 5])
```

All the elements in the array are added by 1 simultaneously. This is very different from Python or most other programming languages. The elements in a NumPy Array all have the same dtype; in the preceding example, this is numpy.int (this is either 32 or 64-bit depending on the machine); therefore, NumPy can save time on checking the type of each element at runtime, which, ordinarily, is done by Python. So, just apply these arithmetic operations:

```
In [4]: y = np.array([-1, 2, 3, 0])
In [5]: x * y
Out[5]: array([-1, 4, 9, 0])
```

so it actually multiplies element-wise, but you don't need to worry specifically about the details of telling it to do things that way

Two NumPy Arrays are multiplied element by element. In the preceding example, two arrays are of equal shape, so no broadcasting is applied here (we will explain different shapes, NumPy Array operations, and broadcasting rules in a later section.) The first element in array x is multiplied by the first element in array y and so on. One important point to note here is that the arithmetic operations between two NumPy Arrays are not matrix multiplications. The result still returns the same shape of NumPy Arrays. A matrix multiplication in NumPy will use numpy.dot(). Take a look at this example:

```
In [6]: np.dot(x, y)
Out[6]: 12
```

NumPy also supports logic comparison between two arrays, and the comparison is vectorized as well. The result returns a Boolean, and NumPy Array indicates which element in both arrays is equal. If two different shapes of arrays are compared, the result would only return one False, which indicates that the two arrays are different, and would really compare each element:

```
In [7]: x == y
Out[7]: array([False, True, True, False], dtype=bool)
```

From the preceding examples, we get an insight into NumPy's element-wise operations, but what's the benefit of using them? How can we know that an optimization has been made through these NumPy operations? We will use the %timeit function in IPython, which was introduced in the last chapter, to show you the difference between NumPy operations and the Python for loop:

```
In [8]: x = np.arange(10000)
In [9]: %timeit x + 1
100000 loops, best of 3: 12.6 µs per loop
In [10]: y = range(10000)
In [11]: %timeit [i + 1 for i in y]
1000 loops, best of 3: 458 µs per loop
```

Two variables, x and y, are the same length and do the same kind of work, which includes adding a value to all the elements in the arrays. With the help of NumPy operations, the performance is way faster than an ordinary Python `for` loop (we use a list comprehension here for neat code, which is faster than an ordinary Python `for` loop, but still, NumPy has better performance when compared to the ordinary Python `for` loop). Knowing this huge distinction can help you speed up your code by replacing your loops with NumPy operations.

As we mentioned in the previous examples, improvement in performance is due to a consistent dtype in a NumPy Array. A tip that can help you use NumPy Arrays correctly is to always consider dtype before you apply any operation, as you will most likely be doing in most programming languages. The following example will show you a hugely different result with the same operation, but this is based on a different dtype array:

```
In [12]: x = np.arange(1,9)
In [13]: x.dtype
Out[13]: dtype('int32')
In [14]: x = x / 10.0          created a new array
In [15]: x
Out[15]: array([ 0.1,  0.2,  0.3,  0.4,  0.5,  0.6,  0.7,  0.8])
In [16]: x.dtype
Out[16]: dtype('float64')
In [17]: y = np.arange(1,9)
In [18]: y /= 10.0          DOES NOT create a new array
In [19]: y
Out[19]: array([0, 0, 0, 0, 0, 0, 0, 0])
In [20]: y.dtype
Out[20]: dtype('int32')
```

The two variables x and y are exactly the same: both are `numpy.int32` Arrays, ranging from *1* to *8* (you might get `numpy.int64` if you use a 64-bit machine) and are divided by `float 10.0`. However, when x is divided by a float, a new NumPy Array is created with `dtype = numpy.float64`. This is a totally new array but has the same variable name, x, so dtype is changed in x. On the other hand, y uses the `/=` sign, which always honors the dtype value of the y array. So, when it is divided by `10.0`, no new array is created; only the value in the element of y is changed but dtype is still `numpy.int32`. This is why x and y end up with two different arrays. Note that, from version of 1.10, NumPy will not allow you to cast the float result as an integer; therefore, `TypeError` will have to be raised.

$x = x /$ and
$x /=$ do not behave the same

Universal functions (ufuncs)

NumPy has many universal functions (so-called ufuncs), so use them to your advantage to eliminate as many loops as you can to optimize your code. The ufuncs have a pretty good coverage in math, trigonometry, summary statistics, and comparison operations. For detailed ufunc lists, refer to the online documentation at
`http://docs.scipy.org/doc/numpy/reference/ufuncs.html`.

Due to the large amount of ufuncs in NumPy, we can hardy cover all of them in a chapter. In this section, we only aim to understand how and why NumPy ufuncs should be used.

Getting started with basic ufuncs

Most ufuncs are either unary or binary, which means that they can take only one or two arguments and apply them, element-wise or in mathematics; this is referred to as a vectorized operation or a NumPy arithmetic operation, which we explained in previous sections. Here are some common ufuncs:

```
In [21]: x = np.arange(5,10)
In [22]: np.square(x)
Out[22]: array([25, 36, 49, 64, 81])
```

Math operations are widely supported in ufuncs, some that are as basic as `numpy.square()` or `numpy.log()`, and others that are advanced trigonometric operations, such as `numpy.arcsin()`, `numpy.rad2deg()`, and more. Here, `np.mod()` retrieves the remainders of division:

```
In [23]: y = np.ones(5) * 10
In [24]: np.mod(y, x)
Out[24]: array([ 0.,   4.,   3.,   2.,   1.])
```

Some ufuncs have similar names, but their function and behaviors are very different. Check online documentation first to make sure you get the result you expect. Here is an example of `numpy.minimum()` and `numpy.min()`:

```
In [25]: np.minimum(x, 7)
Out[25]: array([5, 6, 7, 7, 7])
In [26]: np.min(x)
Out[26]: 5
```

As you can see, `numpy.minimum()` compares two arrays and returns the minimum value for both. 1 is the shape of the array value of which is 7, so it's broadcast to `[7, 7, 7, 7, 7]`. We will talk about the NumPy broadcasting rule in a later section. `numpy.min()`, only takes one required argument and returns the smallest element in the array.

Working with more advanced ufuncs

Most ufuncs have an optional argument to provide more flexibility when using them; the following example will use `numpy.median()`. This is done with an optional `axis` argument on a two-dimensional array created by the `numpy.repeat()` function to repeat the x array three times and assign it to the z variable:

```
In [27]: z = np.repeat(x, 3).reshape(5, 3)
In [28]: z
Out[28]:
array([[5, 5, 5],
       [6, 6, 6],
       [7, 7, 7],
       [8, 8, 8],
       [9, 9, 9]])
In [29]: np.median(z)
Out[29]: 7.0
In [30]: np.median(z, axis = 0)
Out[30]: array([ 7.,   7.,   7.])
In [31]: np.median(z, axis = 1)
Out[31]: array([ 5.,   6.,   7.,   8.,   9.])
```

We can see without applying the `axis` argument that the `numpy.median()` function flattens the array by default and returns a median element, so only one value is returned. With the `axis` argument, if it's applied to 0, the operation will be based on the column; therefore, we obtain a new NumPy Array with a length of 3 (there are 3 columns in total in the z variable). While `axis = 1`, it performed the operation based on rows, so we have a new array with five elements.

ufuncs not only provide optional arguments to tune operations, but many of them also have some built-in methods, which provides even more flexibility. The following example uses `accumulate()` in `numpy.add()` to accumulate the result of applying `add()` to all elements:

```
In [32]: np.add.accumulate(x)
Out[32]: array([ 5, 11, 18, 26, 35])
```

The second example applies the matrix outer operation on `numpy.multiply()` to all pairs of elements from two input arrays. In this example, two arrays are from x. The final shape of the outer product from `multiply()` will be 5 by 5:

```
In [33]: np.multiply.outer(x, x)
Out[33]:
array([[25, 30, 35, 40, 45],
       [30, 36, 42, 48, 54],
       [35, 42, 49, 56, 63],
       [40, 48, 56, 64, 72],
       [45, 54, 63, 72, 81]])
```

If you want something a little more advanced, you will want to consider building your own ufuncs, which might require using the Python- C API, or you may also use Numba modules (vectorize decorators) to implement customized ufuncs. In this chapter, our goal is to understand NumPy ufuncs, so we will not cover customized ufuncs. For further details, refer to NumPy's online documentation, called *Writing your own ufunc*, at `http://docs.scipy.org/doc/numpy/user/c-info.ufunc-tutorial.html`, or a Numba document called *Creating Numpy Universal Functions* at `http://numba.pydata.or g/numba-doc/dev/user/vectorize.html`.

Broadcasting and shape manipulation

NumPy operations are mostly done element-wise, which requires two arrays in an operation to have the same shape; however, this doesn't mean that NumPy operations can't take two differently shaped arrays (refer to the first example we looked at with scalars). NumPy provides the flexibility to broadcast a smaller-sized array across a larger one. But we can't broadcast the array to just about any shape. It needs to follow certain constrains; we will be covering them in this section. One key idea to keep in mind is that broadcasting involves performing meaningful operations over two differently shaped arrays. However, inappropriate broadcasting might lead to an inefficient use of memory that slows down computation.

Broadcasting rules

The general rule for broadcasting is to determine whether two arrays are compatible with dimensioning. There are two conditions that need to be met:

- Two arrays should be of equal dimensions
- One of them is 1

If the preceding conditions are not met, a `ValueError` exception will be thrown to indicate that the arrays have incompatible shapes. Now, we are going through three examples to take a look at how broadcasting rules work:

```
In [35]: x = np.array([[ 0, 0, 0],
    ....:              [10,10,10],
    ....:              [20,20,20]])
In [36]: y = np.array([1, 2, 3])
In [37]: x + y
Out[37]:
array([[ 1,  2,  3],
       [11, 12, 13],
       [21, 22, 23]])
```

Let's make the preceding code into a graph to help us understand broadcasting. The x variable has a shape of (3, 3), while y only has a shape of 3. But in NumPy broadcasting, the shape of y is translated to 3 by 1; therefore, the second condition of the rule has been met. y has been broadcast to the same shape of x by repeating it. The+ operation can apply element-wise.

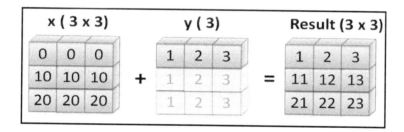

Numpy broadcasting on different shapes of arrays, where x(3,3) + y(3)

Next, we are going to show you the result of broadcasting both arrays:

```
In [38]: x = np.array([[0], [10], [20]])
In [39]: x
Out[39]:
array([[ 0],
       [10],
       [20]])
In [40]: x + y
Out[40]:
array([[ 1,  2,  3],
       [11, 12, 13],
       [21, 22, 23]])
```

The preceding example shows you how both x and y are broadcast. x is broadcast by the column, while y is broadcast by the row since both of them have dimension that are equal to *1* in terms of their shape. The second broadcasting condition has been met, and the new result array is a *3 by 3* array.

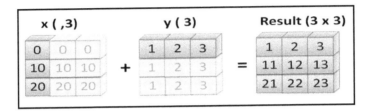

Let's take a look of our last example, which two arrays can't meet the requirement of broadcasting rules:

```
In [41]: x = np.array([[ 0, 0, 0],
    ....:              [10,10,10],
    ....:              [20,20,20]])
In [42]: y = np.arange(1,5)
In [43]: x + y
ValueError: operands could not be broadcast together with shapes (3,3) (4)
```

In the third example, broadcasting can't be performed due to x and y as they have different shapes in the row dimension and none of them are equal to *1*. Thus, none of the broadcasting conditions can be met. NumPy throws ValueError, telling you that the shape is incompatible.

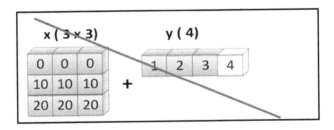

Reshaping NumPy Arrays

After understanding the broadcasting rules, another important concept here is to reshape your NumPy Arrays, especially when you are dealing with multidimensional arrays. It's common for you to create a NumPy Array in just one dimension, reshaping it to a multidimension later, or vice versa. A key idea here is that you can change the shape of your arrays, but the number of elements should not be changed; for example, you can't reshape a *3* by *3* array to a *10* by *1* array. The total number of elements (or a so-called data buffer in the ndarray internal organization) should be consistent before and after reshaping. Or ,you might need to resize, but that's another story. Now, let's look at some shape manipulations:

```
In [44]: x = np.arange(24)
In [45]: x.shape = 2, 3, -1
In [46]: x
Out[46]:
array([[[ 0,  1,  2,  3],
        [ 4,  5,  6,  7],
        [ 8,  9, 10, 11]],
       [[12, 13, 14, 15],
        [16, 17, 18, 19],
        [20, 21, 22, 23]]])
```

The basic reshaping technique changes the `numpy.shape` attribute. In the preceding example, we have an array whose shape is (24,1), and after altering the shape attribute, we obtain an array of the same size but the shape has been changed to *2* by *3* by *4*. Note that *-1* in a shape means the remaining shape size of the transferred array.

```
In [47]: x = np.arange(1000000)
In [48]: x.shape = 100, 100, 100
In [49]: %timeit x.flatten()
1000 loops, best of 3: 1.14 ms per loop
In [50]: %timeit x.ravel()
1000000 loops, best of 3: 330 ns per loop
```

The preceding example is to reshape a *100* by *100* by *100* array back to just one dimension; here, we apply two functions, `numpy.flatten()` and `numpy.ravel()`, to collapse the array, and at the same time, we also compare the execution time. We notice that the speed difference between `numpy.flatten()` and `numpy.ravel()` is huge, but both of them are much faster than three layers of Python looping. The difference in performance between the two functions is that `np.flatten()` creates a copy from the original array, while `np.ravel()` just changes the view (if you don't remember the difference between copies and views, go back a bit to `Chapter 2`, *The NumPy ndarray Object*).

This example simply shows you that NumPy offers many functions and some of them can produce same results; pick up the function that satisfies your purpose and, at the same time, provides you with optimized performance.

Vector stacking

Reshaping changes the shape of one array, but how do we construct a two or multidimensional array by equally-sized row vectors? NumPy provides a solution for this called vector stacking; here, we are going to go through three examples using three different stacking functions to achieve the combination of two arrays based on different dimensions:

```
In [51]: x = np.arange (0, 10, 2)
In [52]: y = np.arange (0, -5, -1)
In [53]: np.vstack ([x, y])
Out[53]:
array([[ 0,  2,  4,  6,  8],
       [ 0, -1, -2, -3, -4]])
```

Numpy.vstack() constructs the new array by vertically stacking two input arrays. The new array is two-dimensional:

```
In [54]: np.hstack ([x, y])
Out[54]: array([ 0,  2,  4,  6,  8,  0, -1, -2, -3, -4])
```

While numpy.hstack() combines the two arrays horizontally, the new array is still one-dimensional:

```
In [55]: np.dstack ([x, y])
Out[55]:
array([[[ 0,  0],
        [ 2, -1],
        [ 4, -2],
        [ 6, -3],
        [ 8, -4]]])
```

numpy.dstack() is a bit different: it stacks the arrays in sequence depth-wise along the third dimension so that the new array is three-dimensional.

In the following code, if you change the array size using `numpy.resize()`, you are enlarging the array, and it will repeat itself until it reaches the new size; otherwise, it will truncate the array to the new size. A point to note here is that `ndarray` also has the `resize()` operation, so you can also use it to change the size of your array by typing `x.resize(8)` in this example; however, you will notice that the enlarging part is filled with zero, not repeating the array itself. Also, you can't use `ndarray.resize()` if you have assigned the array to another variable. `Numpy.resize()` creates a new array with specified shapes, which have fewer limitations than `ndarray.resize()`, and is a more preferable operation to use to change the size of your NumPy Array if necessary:

```
In [56]: x = np.arange(3)
In [57]: np.resize(x, (8,))
Out[57]: array([0, 1, 2, 0, 1, 2, 0, 1])
```

A boolean mask

Indexing and slicing are quite handy and powerful in NumPy, but with the booling mask it gets even better! Let's start by creating a boolean array first. Note that there is a special kind of array in NumPy named a *masked array*. Here, we are not talking about it but we're also going to explain how to extend indexing and slicing with NumPy Arrays:

```
In [58]: x = np.array([1,3,-1, 5, 7, -1])
In [59]: mask = (x < 0)
In [60]: mask
Out[60]: array([False, False,  True, False, False,  True], dtype=bool)
```

We can see from the preceding example that by applying the < logic sign that we applied scalars to a NumPy Array and the naming of a new array to `mask`, it's still vectorized and returns the `True/False` boolean with the same shape of the variable x indicated which element in x meet the criteria:

```
In [61]: x [mask] = 0
In [62]: x
Out[62]: array([1, 3, 0, 5, 7, 0])
```

Using the mask, we gain the ability to access or replace any element value in our arrays without knowing their index. Needless to say, this can be done without using a `for` loop.

The following example shows how to sum up the mask array, where `True` stands for one and `False` stands for 0. We created 50 random values, ranging from to *1*, and 20 of them are larger than *0.5*; however, this is quite expected for a random array:

```
In [69]: x = np.random.random(50)
In [70]: (x > .5).sum()
Out[70]: 20
```

Helper functions

Besides the `help()` and `dir()` functions in Python and other online documentation, NumPy also provides a helper function, `numpy.lookfor()`, to help you find the right function you need. The argument is a string, and it can be in the form of a function name or anything related to it. Let's try to find out more about operations related to `resize`, which we took a look at in an earlier section:

```
In [71]: np.lookfor('resize')
Search results for 'resize'
-------------------------
numpy.ma.resize
    Return a new masked array with the specified size and shape.
numpy.chararray.resize
    Change shape and size of array in-place.
numpy.oldnumeric.ma.resize
    The original array's total size can be any size.
numpy.resize
    Return a new array with the specified shape.
```

Summary

In this chapter, we covered the basic operations of NumPy and its ufuncs. We took a look at the huge difference between NumPy operations and Python looping. We also took a look at how broadcasting works and what we should avoid. We tried to understand the concept of masking as well.

The best way to use NumPy Arrays is to eliminate loops as much as you can and use ufuncs in NumPy instead. Keep in mind the broadcasting rules and use them with care. Using slicing and indexing with masking makes your code more efficient. Most importantly, have fun while using it.

In the next few chapters, we will cover the core libs of NumPy, including date/time and a file I/O to help you extend your NumPy experience.

4

NumPy Core and Libs Submodules

After covering so many NumPy ufuncs in the previous chapter, I hope you still remember the very core of NumPy, which is the ndarray object. We are going to finish the last important attribute of ndarray: strides, which will give you the full picture of memory layout. Also, it's time to show you that NumPy arrays can deal not only with numbers but also with various types of data; we will talk about record arrays and date time arrays. Lastly, we will show how to read/write NumPy arrays from/to files, and start to do some real-world analysis using NumPy.

The topics that will be covered in this chapter are:

- The core of NumPy arrays: memory layout
- Structure arrays (record arrays)
- Date-time in NumPy arrays
- File I/O in NumPy arrays

Introducing strides

Strides are the indexing scheme in NumPy arrays, and indicate the number of bytes to jump to find the next element. We all know the performance improvements of NumPy come from a homogeneous multidimensional array object with fixed-size items, the `numpy.ndarray` object. We've talked about the `shape` (dimension) of the `ndarray` object, the data type, and the order (the C-style row-major indexing arrays and the Fortran style column-major arrays.) Now it's time to take a closer look at **strides**.

Let's start by creating a NumPy array and changing its shape to see the differences in the strides.

1. Create a NumPy array and take a look at the strides:

```
In [1]: import numpy as np
In [2]: x = np.arange(8, dtype = np.int8)
In [3]: x
Out[3]: array([0, 1, 2, 3, 4, 5, 6, 7])
In [4]: x.strides
Out[4]: (1,)
In [5]: str(x.data)
Out[5]: '\x00\x01\x02\x03\x04\x05\x06\x07'
```

A one-dimensional array x is created and its data type is NumPy integer 8, which means each element in the array is an 8-bit integer (1 byte each, and a total of 8 bytes). The strides represent the tuple of bytes to step in each dimension when traversing an array. In the previous example, it's one dimension, so we obtain the tuple as (1,). Each element is 1 byte apart from its previous element. When we print out x.data, we can get the Python buffer object pointing to the start of the data, which is from x01 to x07 in the example.

2. Change the shape and see the stride change:

```
In [6]: x.shape = 2, 4
In [7]: x
Out[7]:
array([[0, 1, 2, 3],
       [4, 5, 6, 7]], dtype=int8)
In [8]: x.strides
Out[8]: (4, 1)
In [9]: str(x.data)
Out[9]: '\x00\x01\x02\x03\x04\x05\x06\x07'
In [10]: x.shape = 1,4,2
In [11]: x.strides
Out[11]: (8, 2, 1)
In [12]: str(x.data)
Out[12]: '\x00\x01\x02\x03\x04\x05\x06\x07'
```

Now we change the dimensions of x to 2 by 4 and check the strides again. We can see it changes to (4, 1), which means the elements in the first dimension are four bytes apart, and the array need to jump four bytes to find the next row, but the elements in the second dimension are still 1 byte apart, jumping one byte to find the next column. Let's print out x.data again, and we can see that the memory layout of the data remains the same, but only the strides change. The same behavior occurs when we change the shape to be three dimensional: 1 by 4 by 2 arrays. (What if our arrays are constructed by the Fortran style order? How will the strides change due to changing the shapes? Try to create a column-major array and do the same exercise to check this out.)

3. So now we know what a stride is, and its relationship to an ndarray object, but how can the stride improve our NumPy experience? Let's do some stride manipulation to get a better sense of this: two arrays are with same content but have different strides:

```
In [13]: x = np.ones((10000,))
In [14]: y = np.ones((10000 * 100, ))[::100]
In [15]: x.shape, y.shape
Out[15]: ((10000,), (10000,))
In [16]: x == y
Out[16]: array([ True,    True,    True, ...,    True,    True,
True], dtype=bool)
```

4. We create two NumPy Arrays, x and y, and do a comparison; we can see that the two arrays are equal. They have the same shape and all the elements are one, but actually the two arrays are different in terms of memory layout. Let's simply use the flags attribute you learned about in Chapter 2, *The NumPy ndarray Object* to check the two arrays' memory layout.

```
In [17]: x.flags
Out[17]: C_CONTIGUOUS : True
          F_CONTIGUOUS : True
          OWNDATA : True
          WRITEABLE : True
          ALIGNED : True
          UPDATEIFCOPY : False

In [18]: y.flags
Out[18]: C_CONTIGUOUS : False
          F_CONTIGUOUS : False
          OWNDATA : False
          WRITEABLE : True
          ALIGNED : True
          UPDATEIFCOPY : False
```

5. We can see that the x array is continuous in both the C and Fortran order while y is not. Let's check the strides for the difference:

```
In [19]: x.strides, y.strides
Out[19]: ((8,), (800,))
```

Array x is created continuously, so in the same dimension each element is eight bytes apart (the default dtype of `numpy.ones` is a 64-bit float); however, y is created from a subset of 10000 * 100 for every 100 elements, so the index schema in the memory layout is not continuous.

6. Even though x and y have the same shape, each element in y is 800 bytes apart from each other. When you use NumPy arrays x and y, you might not notice the difference in indexing, but the memory layout does affect the performance. Let's use the `%timeit` function in IPython to check this out:

```
In [18]: %timeit x.sum()
100000 loops, best of 3: 13.8 µs per loop
In [19]: %timeit y.sum()
10000 loops, best of 3: 25.9 µs per loop
```

Typically with a fixed cache size, when the stride size gets larger, the hit rate (the fraction of memory accessed that finds data in the cache) will be lower, comparatively, while the miss rate (the fraction of memory accessed that has to go to the memory) will be higher. The cache hit time and miss time compose the average data access time. Let's try to look at our example again from the cache perspective. Array x with smaller strides is faster than the larger strides of y. The reason for the difference in performance is that the CPU is pulling data from the main memory to its cache in blocks, and the smaller stride means fewer transfers are needed. See the following graph for details, where the red line represents the size of the CPU cache, and blue boxes represent the memory layout containing the data.

It's obvious that if x and y are both required, 100 blue boxes of data, the required cache time for x will be less.

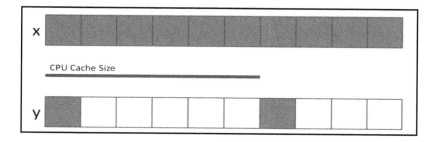

Cache and the x, y array in the memory layout

Structured arrays

Structured arrays or record arrays are useful when you perform computations, and at the same time you could keep closely related data together. For example, when you process incident data and each incident contains geographic coordinates and the occurrence time, while you calculate the final result, you can easily find the associated geographic locations and timepoint for further visualization. NumPy also provides powerful capabilities to create arrays of records, as multiple data types live in one NumPy array. However, one principle in NumPy that still needs to be honored is that the data type in each field (you can think of this as a column in the records) needs to be homogeneous. Here are some simple examples that show you how it works:

```
In [20]: x = np.empty((2,), dtype = ('i4,f4,a10'))
In [21]: x[:] = [(1,0.5, 'NumPy'), (10,-0.5, 'Essential')]
In [22]: x
Out[22]:
array([(1, 0.5, 'NumPy'), (10, -0.5, 'Essential')],
      dtype=[('f0', '<i4'), ('f1', '<f4'), ('f2', 'S10')])
```

In the previous example, we created a one-dimensional record array using numpy.empty() and specified the data types for the elements-the first element is i4 (a 32-bit integer, where i stands for a signed integer, and 4 means 4 bytes, like np.int32), the second element is a 32-bit float (f stands for float and also 4 bytes), and the third element is a string of length less than or equal to 10. We assign the values to the defined array following the data type orders we specified.

You can see the print-out of x, which now contains three different types of records, and we also get a default field name in dtype:f0, f1, and f2. Of course, you may specify your field names, as we'll show you in the following examples.

One thing to note here is that we used the print-out data type-there is a < in front of i4 and f4, and < stands for byteorder *big-endian* (indicating the memory address increase order):

```
In [23]: x[0]
Out[23]: (1, 0.5, 'NumPy')
In [24]: x['f2']
Out[24]:
array(['NumPy', 'Essential'], dtype='|S10')
```

The way we retrieve data remains the same, we use the index to obtain the record, but moreover, we can use the field name to obtain the value of certain fields, so in the previous example, we used f2 to obtain the string field. In the following example, we are going to create a view of x, named y, and see how it interacts with the original record array:

```
In [25]: y = x['f0']
In [26]: y
Out[26]: array([ 1, 10])
In [27]: y[:] = y * 10
In [28]: y
Out[28]: array([ 10, 100])
In [29]: y[:] = y + 0.5
In [30]: y
Out[30]: array([ 10, 100])
In [31]: x
Out[31]:
array([(10, 0.5, 'NumPy'), (100, -0.5, 'Essential')],
      dtype=[('f0', '<i4'), ('f1', '<f4'), ('f2', 'S10')])
```

Here, y is the view of field f0 in x. In the record arrays, the characteristics of NumPy arrays still remain. When you multiply the scalar 10, it still applies to whole array of y (the broadcasting rule), and it always honors the data type. You can see after the multiplication, we add 0.5 to y, but since the data type of field f0 is a 32-bit integer, the result is still [10, 100]. Also, y is a view of f0 in x, so they share the same memory block. When we print out x after the calculation in y, we can find that the values in x have also changed.

Before we go further into the record arrays, let's sort out how to define a record array. The easiest way is as shown in the previous example, where we initialize a NumPy array and use the string argument to specify the data type of fields.

There are many forms of string argument NumPy can accept (see
http://docs.scipy.org/doc/numpy/user/basics.rec.html for details); the most
preferred can be chosen from one of these:

Data types	Representation
b1	Bytes
i1,i2,i4,i8	Signed integers with 1, 2, 4, and 8 bytes corresponding to them
u1,u2,u4,u8	Unsigned integers with 1, 2, 4, and 8 bytes
f2,f4,f8	Floats with 2, 4, and 8 bytes
c8,c16	Complex with 8 and 16 bytes
a<n>	Fixed length strings of length *n*

You may also prefix the string arguments with a repeated number or a shape to define the
dimension of the field, but it's still considered as just one field in the record arrays. Let's try
using the shape as prefix to the string arguments in the following example:

```
In [32]: z = np.ones((2,), dtype = ('3i4, (2,3)f4'))
In [32]: z
Out[32]:
array([([1, 1, 1], [[1.0, 1.0, 1.0], [1.0, 1.0, 1.0]]),
       ([1, 1, 1], [[1.0, 1.0, 1.0], [1.0, 1.0, 1.0]])],
      dtype=[('f0', '<i4', (3,)), ('f1', '<f4', (2, 3))])
```

In the previous example, field f0 is a one-dimensional array with size 3 and f1 is a two-
dimensional array with shape (2, 3). Now, we are clear about the structure of a record
array and how to define it. You might be wondering whether the default field name can be
changed to something meaningful in your analysis? Of course it can! This is how:

```
In [33]: x.dtype.names
Out[33]: ('f0', 'f1', 'f2')
In [34]: x.dtype.names = ('id', 'value', 'note')
In [35]: x
Out[35]:
array([(10, 0.5, 'NumPy'), (100, -0.5, 'Essential')],
      dtype=[('id', '<i4'), ('value', '<f4'), ('note', 'S10')])
```

By assigning the new field names back to the names attribute in the `dtype` object, we can have our customized field names. Or you can do this when you initialize the record arrays by using a list with a tuple, or a dictionary. In the following examples, we are going to create two identical record arrays with customized field names using a list, and a dictionary:

```
In [36]: list_ex = np.zeros((2,), dtype = [('id', 'i4'), ('value', 'f4',
(2,))])
In [37]: list_ex
Out[37]:
array([(0, [0.0, 0.0]), (0, [0.0, 0.0])],
      dtype=[('id', '<i4'), ('value', '<f4', (2,))])
In [38]: dict_ex = np.zeros((2,), dtype = {'names':['id', 'value'],
'formats':['i4', '2f4']})
In [39]: dict_ex
Out[39]:
array([(0, [0.0, 0.0]), (0, [0.0, 0.0])],
      dtype=[('id', '<i4'), ('value', '<f4', (2,))])
```

In the list example, we make a tuple of (field name, data type, and shape) for each field. The shape argument is optional; you may also specify the shape with the data type argument. While using a dictionary to define the field, there are two required keys (`names` and `formats`) and each key has an equally sized list of values.

Before we go on to the next section, we are going to show you how to access multiple fields in your record array all at once. The following example still uses the array x that we created at beginning with a customized field: id, value, and note:

```
In [40]: x[['id', 'note']]
Out[40]:
array([(10, 'NumPy'), (100, 'Essential')],
      dtype=[('id', '<i4'), ('note', 'S10')])
```

You may find this example too simple; if so, you can try to create a new record array from a real-life example containing the country name, population, and rank using the data from Wikipedia:
`https://en.wikipedia.org/wiki/List_of_countries_and_dependencies_by_pop ulation`. This will be more fun!

Dates and time in NumPy

Dates and times are important when you are doing time series analytics, from something as simple as accumulating daily visitors in a museum to something as complicated as trending regression for a crime forecast. Starting from NumPy 1.7, the NumPy core supports date time types (though it's still experimental, and might be subject to change). In order to differentiate from the datetime object in Python, the data type is called datetime64.

This section will cover numpy.datetime64 creation, time delta arithmetic, and the conversion between units and the Python datetime. Let's create a numpy.datetime64 object by using an ISO string:

```
In [41]: x = np.datetime64('2015-04-01')
In [42]: y = np.datetime64('2015-04')
In [43]: x.dtype, y.dtype
Out[43]: (dtype('<M8[D]'), dtype('<M8[M]'))
```

x and y are both numpy.datetime64 objects and are constructed from an ISO 8601 string (the universal date format-for details see https://en.wikipedia.org/wiki/ISO_8601). But the input string for x contains a days unit while the string for y does not. While creating the NumPy datetime64, it will automatically select from the form of the input string, so when we print out the dtype for both x and y, we can see that x with unit D stands for days while y with unit M stands for months. The< is also the byteorder, here it is the big-endian, and M8 is the short notation of datetime64 (implemented from np.int64). The default date units supported by numpy.datetime64 are years (Y), months (M), weeks (W), and days (D), while the time units are hours (h), minutes (m), seconds (s), and milliseconds (ms).

Of course we can specify the units when we create the array and also use the numpy.arange() method to create the sequence of the array. See the following examples:

```
In [44]: y = np.datetime64('2015-04', 'D')
In [45]: y, y.dtype
Out[45]: (numpy.datetime64('2015-04-01'), dtype('<M8[D]'))
In [46]: x = np.arange('2015-01', '2015-04', dtype = 'datetime64[M]')
In [47]: x
Out[47]: array(['2015-01', '2015-02', '2015-03'], dtype='datetime64[M]')
```

However, it's not allowed to specify a time unit when the ISO string only contains date units. A TypeError will be triggered, since conversion between date units and time units requires a choice of time zone and the particular time of day on a given date:

```
In [48]: y = np.datetime64('2015-04-01', 's')
TypeError: Cannot parse "2015-04-01" as unit 's' using casting rule
'same_kind'
```

Next, we are going to do a subtraction of two `numpy.datetime64` arrays, and you will see that the broadcasting rules are still valid as long as the date/time units between two arrays are convertible. We use the same array x created earlier and create a new y for the following example:

```
In [49]: x
Out[49]: array(['2015-01', '2015-02', '2015-03'], dtype='datetime64[M]')
In [50]: y = np.datetime64('2015-01-01')
In [51]: x - y
Out[51]: array([ 0, 31, 59], dtype='timedelta64[D]')
```

Interestingly enough, the result array of x subtracting y is [0, 31, 59], not the date anymore, and the `dtype` has changed to `timedelta64[D]`. Because NumPy doesn't have a physical quantities system in its core, the `timedelta64` data type was created to complement `datetime64`. In the previous example, [0, 31, 59] is the units from 2015-01-01 in each element in x, and the units are days (D). You may also do the arithmetic between `datetime64` and `timedelta64`, as shown in the following examples:

```
In [52]: np.datetime64('2015') + np.timedelta64(12, 'M')
Out[52]: numpy.datetime64('2016-01')
In [53]: np.timedelta64(1, 'W') / np.timedelta64(1, 'D')
Out[53]: 7.0
```

In the last part of this section, we are going to talk about the conversion between `numpy.datetime64` and Python the `datetime`. Although the `datetime64` object inherits many traits from a NumPy array, there are still some benefits from using the Python `datetime` object (such as the `date` and `year` attributes, `isoformat`, and more) or vice versa. For example, you may have a list of `datetime` objects, and you may want to convert them to `numpy.datetime64` for the arithmetic or other NumPy ufuncs. In the following example, we are going to convert the existing `datetime64` array x to a list of Python `datetime` in two ways:

```
In [54]: x
Out[54]: array(['2015-01', '2015-02', '2015-03'], dtype='datetime64[M]')
In [55]: x.tolist()
Out[55]:
[datetime.date(2015, 1, 1),
 datetime.date(2015, 2, 1),
 datetime.date(2015, 3, 1)]
In [56]: [element.item() for element in x]
Out[56]:
[datetime.date(2015, 1, 1),
 datetime.date(2015, 2, 1),
 datetime.date(2015, 3, 1)]
```

We can see that `numpy.datetime64.tolist()` and `numpy.datetime64.item()` with the `for` loop can achieve the same goal, that is, converting the array to a list of Python `datetime` objects. But needless to say, we all know which is the more preferred method to do the conversion (if you don't know the answer, have a quick look at Chapter 3, *Using NumPy Arrays*.) On the other hand, if you already have a list of Python `datetime` and want to convert it to NumPy `datetime64` arrays, simply use the `numpy.array()` function.

File I/O and NumPy

Now we have the ability to perform NumPy array computation and manipulation and we know how to construct a record array, it's time for us to do some real-world analysis by reading files into a NumPy array and outputing the result array to a file for further analysis.

We should talk about reading the file first and then exporting the file. But now, we are going to reverse the process, and create a record array first and then output the array to a CSV file. We read the exported CSV file into the NumPy record arrays and compared it with our original record array. The sample array we're going to create will contain an `id` field with consecutive integers, a `value` field containing random floats, and a `date` field with `numpy.datetime64['D']`. This exercise will use all the knowledge you gained from the previous sections and chapters. Let's start creating the record array:

```
In [57]: id = np.arange(1000)
In [58]: value = np.random.random(1000)
In [59]: day = np.random.random_integers(0, 365, 1000) *
np.timedelta64(1,'D')
In [60]: date = np.datetime64('2014-01-01') + day
In [61]: rec_array = np.core.records.fromarrays([id, value, date],
names='id, value, date', formats='i4, f4, a10')
In [62]: rec_array[:5]
Out[62]:
rec.array([(0, 0.07019801437854767, '2014-07-10'),
       (1, 0.4863224923610687, '2014-12-03'),
       (2, 0.9525277614593506, '2014-03-11'),
       (3, 0.39706873893737793, '2014-01-02'),
       (4, 0.8536589741706848, '2014-09-14')],
      dtype=[('id', '<i4'), ('value', '<f4'), ('date', 'S10')])
```

We first create three NumPy arrays representing the fields we need: `id`, `value`, and `date`. When creating the `date` field, we combine the `numpy.datetime64` with a random NumPy array with size `1000` to simulate random dates in the range from `2014-01-01` to `2014-12-31` (365 days).

Then we use the `numpy.core.records.fromarrays()` function to merge the three arrays into one record array and assign the `names` (field name) and the `formats` (data type). One thing to notice here is that the record array doesn't support the `numpy.datetime64` object, so we stored it in the array as a date/time string with a length of 10.

If you are using Python 3, you will find a prefix b added to the front of the date/time string in the record array such as b`'2014-09-25'`. b here stands for "bytes literals" meaning it only contains ASCII characters (all string types in Python 3 are Unicode ,which is one major change between Python 2 and 3). Therefore in Python 3, converting an object (`datetime64`) to a string will add the prefix to differentiate between the normal string type. However, it doesn't affect what we are going to do next-exporting the record array to a CSV file:

```
In [63]: np.savetxt('./record.csv', rec_array, fmt='%i,%.4f,%s')
```

We use the `numpy.savetxt()` function to handle the exporting, and we specify the first argument as the exported file location, the array name, and the format using the `fmt` argument. We have three fields with three different data types and we want to add , in between each field in the CSV file. If you prefer any other delimiters, replace the comma in the `fmt` argument. We also get rid of redundant digits in the `value` field, so we specify only four digits after the decimal points to the file by using `%.4f`. Now you may go to the file location we specified in the first argument to check the CSV file. Open it in a spreadsheet software program and you can see the following:

	A	B	C
1	0	0.0702	7/10/2014
2	1	0.4863	12/3/2014
3	2	0.9525	3/11/2014
4	3	0.3971	1/2/2014
5	4	0.8537	9/14/2014

Next, we are going to read the CSV file to a record array and use the `value` field to generate a mask field, named `mask`, which represents a value larger than or equal to 0.75. Then we will append the new mask field to the record array. Let's read the CSV file first:

```
In [64]: read_array = np.genfromtxt('./record.csv', dtype='i4,f4,a10',
delimiter=',', skip_header=0)
In [65]: read_array[:5]
Out[65]:
array([[(0, 0.07020000368356705, '2014-07-10'),
```

```
     (1, 0.486299991607666, '2014-12-03'),
     (2, 0.9524999856948853, '2014-03-11'),
     (3, 0.3971000015735626, '2014-01-02'),
     (4, 0.8536999821662903, '2014-09-14')],
   dtype=[('f0', '<i4'), ('f1', '<f4'), ('f2', 'S10')])
```

We use `numpy.genfromtxt()` to read the file into NumPy record array. The first argument is still the file location we want to access, and the `dtype` argument is optional. If we didn't specify this, NumPy will determine the `dtype` argument using the contents of each column individually. Since we clearly know about the data, it's recommended to specify every time when you read the file.

The `delimiter` argument is also optional, and by default, any consecutive whitespaces act as delimiters. However, we used ", "for the CSV file. The last optional argument we use in the method is the `skip_header`. Although we didn't have the field name on top of the records in the file, NumPy provides the functionality to skip a number of lines at the beginning of the file.

Other than `skip_header`, the `numpy.genfromtext()` function supports 22 more operation parameters to fine-tune the array, such as defining missing and filling values. For more details, please refer to http://docs.scipy.org/doc/numpy-1.10.0/reference/generated/numpy.genfromtxt.html.

Now the data is read in to the record array, you will find that the second field is more than four digits after the decimal points as we specified in exporting the CSV. The reason for this is because we use `f4` as its data type when read in. The empty digits will be filled by NumPy, but the valid four digits remain the same as in the file. You may also notice we lost the field name, so let's specify it:

```
In [66]: read_array.dtype.names = ('id', 'value', 'date')
```

The last part of this exercise is to create a mask variable with values based on the `value` field larger than or equal to `0.75`. We append the new mask array to the `read_array` as a new column:

```
In [68]: mask = read_array['value'] >= 0.75
In [69]: from numpy.lib.recfunctions import append_fields
In [70]: read_array = append_fields(read_array, 'mask', data=mask,
dtypes='i1')
In [71]: read_array[:5]
Out[71]:
masked_array(data = [(0, 0.07020000368356705, '2014-07-10', 0)
  (1, 0.486299991607666, '2014-12-03', 0)
```

```
(2, 0.9524999856948853, '2014-03-11', 1)
(3, 0.3971000015735626, '2014-01-02', 0)
dtype = [('id', '<i4'), ('value', '<f4'), ('date', 'S10'), ('mask','i1')])
```

numpy.lib.recfunctions can only be accessed when you import it directly, and the append_field() function is in the module. Appending a record array is as simple as appending a NumPy array: the first argument is the base array; the second argument is the new field name mask, and the data associated with it; and the last argument is the data type. Because a mask is a Boolean array, NumPy will apply the mask automatically to the record array, but we can still see a new field added to the read_array and the value of the mask reflects the value threshold (>= 0.75) in the value field. This is just the beginning of showing you how to hook up NumPy array with your data file. Now it's time to do some real analysis with your data!

Summary

In this chapter, we covered the last important component of the ndarray object: strides. We saw a huge difference in memory layouts and also in performance when you use different ways to initialize your NumPy array. We also got to know the record array (structured array) and how to manipulate the date/time in NumPy. Most importantly, we saw how to read and write our data with NumPy.

NumPy is powerful not only because of its performance or ufuncs, but also because of how easy it can make your analysis. Use NumPy with your data as much as you can!

Next, we will look at linear algebra and matrix computation using NumPy.

5

Linear Algebra in NumPy

NumPy is designed for numeric computations; underneath the hood it is still the powerful `ndarray` object, but at the same time NumPy provides different types of objects to solve mathematical problems. In this chapter, we will cover the matrix object and polynomial object to help you solve problems using a non-ndarray way. Again, NumPy provides a lot of standard mathematical algorithms and supports multi-dimensional data. While a matrix can't perform three-dimensional data, using the `ndarray` objects with the NumPy functions of linear algebra and polynomials is more preferable (the extensive SciPy library is another good choice for linear algebra, but NumPy is our focus in this book). Let's use NumPy to do some math now!

The topics that will be covered in this chapter are:

- Matrix and vector operations
- Decompositions
- Mathematics of polynomials
- Regression and curve fitting

The matrix class

For linear algebra, using matrices might be more straightforward. The matrix object in NumPy inherits all the attributes and methods from `ndarray`, but it's strictly two-dimensional, while `ndarray` can be multi-dimensional. The well-known advantage of using NumPy matrices is that they provide matrix multiplication as the * notation; for example, if x and y are matrices, x * y is their matrix product. However, starting from Python 3.5/NumPy 1.10, native matrix multiplication is supported with the new operator "

However, starting from Python 3.5/NumPy 1.10, native matrix multiplication is supported with the new operator "@". So that is one more good reason to use ndarray (https://docs.python.org/3/whatsnew/3.5.html#whatsnew-pep-465).

However, matrix objects still provide convenient conversion such as inverse and conjugate transpose while an ndarraydoes not. Let's start by creating NumPy matrices:

```
In [1]: import numpy as np
In [2]: ndArray = np.arange(9).reshape(3,3)
In [3]: x = np.matrix(ndArray)
In [4]: y = np.mat(np.identity(3))
In [5]: x
Out[5]:
matrix([[0, 1, 2],
        [3, 4, 5],
        [6, 7, 8]])
In [6]: y
Out[6]:
matrix([[1., 0., 0.],
        [0., 1., 0.],
        [0., 0., 1.]])
```

There are a couple of ways to create or convert to a NumPy matrix object, and the more preferred way is to use numpy.mat() or numpy.matrix(). Both methods create matrices, but numpy.matrix() creates a copy while numpy.mat() changes the view only; it's equivalent to numpy.matrix(data, copy = False). In the previous example, we create two matrices, both of which are from the ndarray object (the np.identity(3) returns a 3 x 3 identity array). Of course you can use a string or list to create a matrix, for example: np.matrix('0 1 2; 3 4 5; 6 7 8'),
and np.matrix([[0,1,2],[3,4,5],[6,7,8]]) will create the same matrix as x. In the following example, we are going to do some basic matrix operations:

```
In [7]: x + y
Out[7]:
matrix([[ 1.,  1.,  2.],
        [ 3.,  5.,  5.],
        [ 6.,  7.,  9.]])
In [8]: x * x
Out[8]:
matrix([[ 15,  18,  21],
        [ 42,  54,  66],
        [ 69,  90, 111]])
In [9]: np.dot(ndArray, ndArray)
Out[9]:
array([[ 15,  18,  21],
       [ 42,  54,  66],
```

```
            [ 69,   90,  111]])
In [10]: x**3
Out[10]:
matrix([[ 180,   234,   288],
        [ 558,   720,   882],
        [ 936,  1206,  1476]])
In [11]: z = np.matrix(np.random.random_integers(1, 50, 9).reshape(3,3))
In [12]: z
Out[12]:
matrix([[32, 21, 28],
        [ 2, 24, 22],
        [32, 20, 22]])
In [13]: z.I
Out[13]:
matrix( [[-0.0237 -0.0264  0.0566]
         [-0.178   0.0518  0.1748]
         [ 0.1963 -0.0086 -0.1958]])

In [14]: z.H
Out[14]:
matrix([[32   2 32]
        [21 24 20]
        [28 22 22]])
```

You can see from the previous example that, when we use the * notation, it applies the matrix multiplication as you use numpy.dot() for ndarray (we will talk about this in the next section). Also, the ** power notation is done in a matrix way. We also created a matrix z from random functions to show when the matrix is invertible (not singular). You can obtain the inverse matrix using numpy.matrix.I. We can also do a conjugate (Hermitian) transpose using numpy.matrix.H.

Now we know how to create a matrix object and do some basic operations, it's time for some practice. Let's try to solve a simple linear equation. Suppose we have a linear equation as $A x = b$ and we want to know the value of x. A possible solution will be as follows:

```
A-1A x = A-1 b
I x = A-1 b
x = A-1 b
```

We obtain x by multiplying the inverse of A and b, so let's do this with numpy.matrix:

```
In [15]: A = np.mat('3 1 4; 1 5 9; 2 6 5')
In [16]: b = np.mat([[1],[2],[3]])
In [17]: x = A.I * b
In [18]: x
Out[18]:
matrix([[ 0.2667],
```

```
      [ 0.4667],
      [-0.0667]])
In [21]: np.allclose(A * x, b)
Out[21]: True
```

We obtained x, and we used `numpy.allclose()` to compare the LHS and the RHS within a tolerance. The default absolute tolerance is `1e-8`. The result returns `True`, meaning that LHS and RHS are equal within the tolerance, which verifies our solution.

Though `numpy.matrix()` takes an ordinary matrix form, in most cases `ndarray` would be good enough for you to do linear algebra. Now we will simply compare the performance between `ndarray` and `matrix`:

```
In [20]: x = np.arange(25000000).reshape(5000,5000)

In [21]: y = np.mat(x)

In [22]: %timeit x.T
10000000 loops, best of 3: 176 ns per loop

In [23]: %timeit y.T
1000000 loops, best of 3: 1.36 µs per loop
```

This example shows a huge performance difference between `ndarray` and `matrix` when doing a transpose. Both x and y have 5,000 by 5,000 elements, but x is a two-dimensional `ndarray`, while y converted it to the same shape `matrix`. The NumPy matrix will always do operations in the matrix way, even if the computation has been optimized by NumPy.

While `ndarray` here by default reverses the dimensions instead of permuting the axes (the matrix always permutes the axes), that's a huge performance improvement trick done in `ndarray`. Therefore, `ndarray` is preferred when doing linear algebra especially for large sets of data considering its performance. Use `matrix` only when necessary. Before we go on to the next section, let's go through two more `matrix` object properties that convert a `matrix` to a basic `ndarray`:

```
In [24]: A.A
Out[24]:
array([[3, 1, 4],
       [1, 5, 9],
       [2, 6, 5]])
In [25]: A.A1
Out[25]: array([3, 1, 4, 1, 5, 9, 2, 6, 5])
```

The previous examples use the matrix A we created in the linear equation practice. `numpy.matrix.A` returns the basic `ndarray` and `numpy.matrix.A1` returns a one-dimensional `ndarray`.

Linear algebra in NumPy

Before we get into linear algebra class in NumPy, there are five vector products we will cover at the beginning of this section. Let's review them one by one, starting with the `numpy.dot()` product:

```
In [26]: x = np.array([[1, 2], [3, 4]])
In [27]: y = np.array([[10, 20], [30, 40]])
In [28]: np.dot(x, y)
Out[28]:
array([[ 70, 100],
       [150, 220]])
```

The `numpy.dot()` function performs matrix multiplication, and the detailed calculation is shown here:

$$\begin{bmatrix} 1*10+2*30 & 1*20+2*40 \\ 3*10+4*30 & 3*20+4*40 \end{bmatrix} = \begin{bmatrix} 70 & 100 \\ 150 & 220 \end{bmatrix}$$

`numpy.vdot()` handles multi-dimensional arrays differently than `numpy.dot()`. It does not perform a matrix product, but flattens input arguments to one-dimensional vectors first:

```
In [29]: np.vdot(x, y)
Out[29]: 300
```

The detailed calculation of `numpy.vdot()` is as follows:

$$1*10+2*20+3*30+4*40 = 300$$

The `numpy.outer()` function is the outer product of two vectors. It flattens the input arrays if they are not one-dimensional. Let's say that the flattened input vector A has shape `(M, )` and the flattened input vector B has shape `(N, )`. Then the result shape would be `(M, N)`:

```
In [100]: np.outer(x,y)
Out[100]:
array([[ 10,  20,  30,  40],
       [ 20,  40,  60,  80],
       [ 30,  60,  90, 120],
       [ 40,  80, 120, 160]])
```

The detailed calculation of `numpy.outer()` is as follows:

$$
\begin{bmatrix}
1*10 & 1*20 & 1*30 & 1*40 \\
2*10 & 2*20 & 2*30 & 2*40 \\
3*10 & 3*20 & 3*30 & 3*40 \\
4*10 & 4*20 & 4*30 & 4*40
\end{bmatrix}
=
\begin{bmatrix}
10 & 20 & 30 & 40 \\
20 & 40 & 60 & 80 \\
30 & 60 & 90 & 120 \\
40 & 80 & 120 & 160
\end{bmatrix}
$$

The last one is the `numpy.cross()` product, a binary operation of two vectors (and it can only work for vectors) in three-dimensional space, the result of which is a vector perpendicular to both input data (a,b). If you are not familiar with the outer product, please refer to `https://en.wikipedia.org/wiki/Cross_product`. The following example shows that a and b are arrays of vectors, and the cross product of (a,b) and (b,a):

```
In [31]: a = np.array([1,0,0])
In [32]: b = np.array([0,1,0])
In [33]: np.cross(a,b)
Out[33]: array([0, 0, 1])
In [34]: np.cross(b,a)
Out[34]: array([ 0,  0, -1])
```

A detailed calculation is shown in the following graph, and the cross-product of two vectors a and b is denoted by *a x b*:

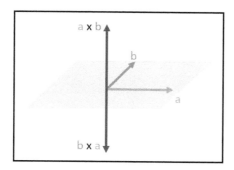

The previous functions are provided by NumPy for standard vector routines. Now we are going to talk about the key topic of this section: the numpy.linalg sub-modules for linear algebra. Using the NumPy ndarray with numpy.linalg would be better than using numpy.matrix().

 If you have scipy as a dependency to your program, scipy.linalg has more advanced functions such as trigonometric functions in matrix, and more decomposition choices than numpy.linalg. However, NumPy includes all the basic operations.

In the following examples, we will go through the rest of the basic operations of numpy.linalg and use them to solve the linear equation in the matrix section:

```
In [35]: x = np.array([[4,8],[7,9]])
In [36]: np.linalg.det(x)
Out[36]: -20.000000000000007
```

The previous example computes the determinant of a square array. Of course we can use numpy.linalg.inv() to compute the inverse of an array, just as we use numpy.matrix.I:

```
In [37]: np.linalg.inv(x)
Out[37]:
array([[-0.45,   0.4 ],
       [ 0.35,  -0.2 ]])
In [38]: np.mat(x).I
Out[38]:
matrix([[-0.45,   0.4 ],
        [ 0.35,  -0.2 ]])
```

From the previous example, we can see that `numpy.linalg.inv()` provides an identical result to `numpy.matrix.I`. The only difference is that `numpy.linalg` returns `ndarray`. Next, we will go back to the linear equation *A x = b* again, to see how we can use `numpy.linalg.solve()` to achieve the same result as using the matrix object:

```
In [39]: x = np.linalg.solve(A,b)
In [40]: x
Out[40]:
matrix([[ 0.2667],
        [ 0.4667],
        [-0.0667]])
```

`numpy.linalg.solve(A,b)` computes the solution for x, where the first input parameter (A) stands for the coefficient array and the second parameter (b) stands for the coordinate or dependent variable values. The `numpy.linalg.solve()` function honored the input data type. In the example, we use matrices as input, so the output also returns a matrix x. We can also use the `ndarray` as our inputs.

When doing linear algebra with NumPy, it's better to use only one data type, either `ndarray` or `matrix`. It's not recommended to have a mixed type in the calculation. One reason is to reduce the conversion between different data types; the other reason is to avoid unexpected errors in the computation with two types. Since `ndarray` has fewer restrictions on data dimensions and can perform all matrix-like operations, using `ndarray` with `numpy.linalg`, is preferred over `matrix`.

Decomposition

There are there decompositions provided by `numpy.linalg` and in this section, we will cover two that are the most commonly used: **singular value decomposition** (**svd**) and **QR** factorization. Let's start by computing the **eigenvalues** and **eigenvectors** first. Before we get started, if you are not familiar with eigenvalues and eigenvectors, you may review them at `https://en.wikipedia.org/wiki/Eigenvalues_and_eigenvectors`. Let's start:

```
In [41]: x = np.random.randint(0, 10, 9).reshape(3,3)
In [42]: x
Out[42]:
array([[ 1,  5,  0]
       [ 7,  4,  0]
       [ 2,  9,  8]])
In [42]: w, v = np.linalg.eig(x)
In [43]: w
Out[43]: array([ 8.,  8.6033,  -3.6033])
In [44]: v
```

```
Out[44]:
array([[ 0.,   0.0384,   0.6834]
       [ 0.,   0.0583,  -0.6292]
       [ 1.,   0.9976,   0.3702]]
)
```

In the previous example, first we created a 3 x 3 `ndarray` using `numpy.random.randint()` and we computed the eigenvalues and eigenvectors using `np.linalg.eig()`. The function returns two tuples: the first one is the eigenvalues, each repeated according to its multiplicity, and the second one is the normalized eigenvectors, in which column `v[: , i]` is the eigenvector corresponding to the eigenvalue `w[i]`. In this example, we unpacked the tuples into `w` and `v`. If the input `ndarray` is complex-valued, the computed eigenvectors would be the complex type too, as you can see in the following example:

```
In [45]: y = np.array([[1, 2j],[-3j, 4]])
In [46]: np.linalg.eig(y)
Out[46]:
(array([ -0.3723+0.j,   5.3723+0.j]),
 array([[0.8246+0.j     ,   0.0000+0.416j    ],
        [-0.0000+0.5658j,   0.9094+0.j    ]]))
```

But if the input `ndarray` is real, the computed eigenvalues would also be real; therefore, when computing, we should be careful of rounding errors, as you can see in the following example:

```
In [47]: z = np.array([[1 + 1e-10, -1e-10],[1e-10, 1 - 1e-10]])
In [48]: np.linalg.eig(z)
Out[48]:
(array([ 1.,   1.]), array([[0.70710678,   0.707106],
        [0.70710678,   0.70710757]]))
```

`ndarrayz` is the real type (`numpy.float64`), so when computing the eigenvalues it will automatically round off. In theory, the eigenvalues should be *1 +/- 1e-10*, but you can see from the first `np.linalg.eig()` that the eigenvalues are both rounding up to *1*.

`svd` can be thought of as an extension of the eigenvalue. We can use `numpy.linalg.svd()` to decompose an M x N array, so let's start with a simple example:

```
In [51]: np.set_printoptions(precision = 4)
In [52]: A = np.array([3,1,4,1,5,9,2,6,5]).reshape(3,3)
In [53]: u, sigma, vh = np.linalg.svd(A)
In [54]: u
Out[54]:
array([[-0.3246,   0.799 ,   0.5062],
       [-0.7531,   0.1055,  -0.6494],
```

```
            [-0.5723, -0.592 ,  0.5675]])
In [55]: vh
Out[55]:
array([[-0.2114, -0.5539, -0.8053],
       [ 0.4633, -0.7822,  0.4164],
       [ 0.8606,  0.2851, -0.422 ]])
In [56]: sigma
Out[56]: array([ 13.5824,   2.8455,   2.3287])
```

In this example, `numpy.linalg.svd()` returned three tuples of arrays and we unpacked it into three variables: u, `sigma`, and vh, in which u stands for the left-singular vectors of A (eigenvectors of *AA-1*), vh is the inverse matrix of the right singular vectors of A (eigenvectors of *(A-1A) -1*), and `sigma` is the non-zero singular values of A (eigenvalues of both *AA-1* and *A-1A*). In the example, there are three eigenvalues and they were returned in order. You might be suspicious about the result, so let's do some math to verify it:

```
In [57]: diag_sigma = np.diag(sigma)
In [58]: diag_sigma
Out[58]:
array([[ 13.5824,    0.   ,    0.   ],
       [  0.   ,    2.8455,    0.   ],
       [  0.   ,    0.   ,    2.3287]])
In [59]: Av = u.dot(diag_sigma).dot(vh)
In [60]: Av
Out[60]:
array([[ 3.,   1.,   4.],
       [ 1.,   5.,   9.],
       [ 2.,   6.,   5.]])
In [61]: np.allclose(A, Av)
Out[61]: True
```

The input array A can be translated to $U \sum V^*$ in svd, where $\sum$ is the vector of singular values. However, the returned sigma from NumPy is an array with non-zero values, and we need to make it into a vector, so in this example the shape would be (3,3). We first use `numpy.diag()` to make sigma a diagonal matrix called `diag_sigma`. Then we just perform a matrix multiplication between u, `diag_sigma`, and vh, to check that the calculated result (Av) is identical to the original input A, meaning we verified the svd result.

QR decomposition, sometimes called polar decomposition, works for any M x N array and decomposes it into an orthogonal matrix (Q) and an upper triangular matrix (R). Let's try to use it to solve the previous *Ax = b* problem:

```
In [62]: b = np.array([1,2,3]).reshape(3,1)
In [63]: q, r = np.linalg.qr(A)
In [64]: x = np.dot(np.linalg.inv(r), np.dot(q.T, b))
In [65]: x
```

```
Out[65]:
array([[ 0.2667],
       [ 0.4667],
       [-0.0667]])
```

We decomposed A using `numpy.linalg.qr()` to obtain q and r. So now the original equation is translated into *(q * r)x = b*. We can obtain x using matrix multiplication (the dot product) of inverse r and inverse q and b. Since q is a unitary matrix, we used transpose instead of inverse. As you can see, the result x is the same as when we used matrix and `numpy.linalg.solve()`; it's just another way to solve the linear problem.

 In general, the calculation of the inverse of the triangular matrix is much more efficient, as you can create a large dataset and compare the performance between different solutions.

Polynomial mathematics

NumPy also provides methods to work with polynomials, and includes a package called `numpy.polynomial` to create, manipulate, and fit the polynomials. A common application of this would be interpolation and extrapolation. In this section, our focus is still on using ndarray with NumPy functions instead of using polynomial instances. (Don't worry, we will still show you the usage of the polynomial class.)

As we stated in the matrix class section, using ndarray with NumPy functions is preferred since ndarray can be accepted in any functions while matrix and polynomial objects need to be converted, especially when communicating to other programs. Both of them provided handy properties, but in most cases ndarray would be good enough.

In this section, we will cover how to calculate the coefficients based on a set of roots, and how to solve a polynomial equation, and finally we will evaluate integrals and derivatives. Let's start by calculating the coefficients of a polynomial:

```
In [66]: root = np.array([1,2,3,4])
In [67]: np.poly(root)
Out[67]: array([  1, -10,   35, -50,   24])
```

`numpy.poly()` returned a one-dimensional array of polynomial coefficients whose roots are the given array `root` from the highest to lowest exponents. In this example, we take the root array $[1,2,3,4]$ and return the polynomial, which is equivalent to $x4 - 10×3 + 35×2 - 50x + 24$.

One thing we need be careful about is that the input roots array should be a one-dimensional or square two-dimensional array, or a `ValueError` will be triggered. Of course, we can also perform the opposite operation: calculating the roots based on the coefficients using `numpy.roots()`:

```
In [68]: np.roots([1,-10,35,-50,24])
Out[68]: array([ 4.,   3.,   2.,   1.])
```

Now, let's say we have the equation $y = x4 - 10×3 + 35×2 - 50x + 24$, and we want to know the value of y when $x = 5$. We can use `numpy.polyval()` to calculate this:

```
In [69]: np.polyval([1,-10,35,-50,24], 5)
Out[69]: 24
```

`numpy.polyval()` takes two input parameters, the first being the coefficient array of the polynomial, and the second one being the specific point value to evaluate the given polynomial. We can also input a sequence of x, and the result will return an `ndarray` whose values correspond to the given x sequence.

Next we will talk about **integrals** and **derivatives**. We will continue the example of $x^4 - 10x^3 + 35x^2 - 50x + 24$:

```
In [70]: coef = np.array([1,-10,35,-50,24])
In [71]: integral = np.polyint(coef)
In [72]: integral
Out[72]: array([ 0.2 ,   -2.5 ,   11.6667,  -25.  ,   24.  ,   0.  ])
In [73]: np.polyder(integral) == coef
Out[73]: array([ True,   True,   True,   True,   True], dtype=bool)
In [74]: np.polyder(coef, 5)
Out[74]: array([], dtype=int32)
```

In this example, we use `numpy.polyint()` for the integral calculus and the result is equivalent to:

$$\frac{1}{5}x^5 - \frac{1}{4}x^4 + \frac{35}{3}x^3 - 25x^2 + 24x$$

The default integration constant is 0, but we can specify it using the input parameter `k`. You can do some exercises on this by yourself for the integral of a different `k`.

Let's go back to the previous example-after doing the integration, we performed the differential calculus right away using `numpy.polyder()` and we compared the derivatives to the original `coef` array. We got five `True` boolean arrays, which verified that both are identical.

We can also specify the order of differentiation (the default is 1) in `numpy.polyder()`. As we expected, when we calculate the fifth-order derivative of a fourth-order polynomial, it returns an empty array.

Now we will repeat these examples using an instance of the polynomial class to see the differences in the usage. The very first step in using the `numpy.polynomial` class is to initialize a polynomial instance. Let's start:

```
In [75]: from numpy.polynomial import polynomial
In [76]: p = polynomial.Polynomial(coef)
In [77]: p
Out[77]: Polynomial([  1., -10.,   35., -50.,   24.], [-1,  1], [-1,  1])
```

Note that beside the returned type of `p` is an instance of the class `Polynomial`, and there are three parts returned. The first part is the coefficient of the polynomial. The second one is `domain`, which represents the input value interval in the polynomial (the default is `[-1, 1]`). And the third one is `window`, which maps the domain interval to the corresponding interval based on the polynomial (the default is also `[-1, 1]`):

```
In [78]: p.coef
Out[78]: array([  1., -10.,   35., -50.,   24.])
In [79]: p.roots()
Out[79]: array([ 0.25  ,  0.3333,  0.5   ,  1.    ])
```

With the `Polynomial` instance, we can simply call the `coef` property to show the `ndarray` of the coefficient. The `roots()` method will show the roots. Next we will evaluate the polynomial of a specific value, 5:

```
In [80]: polynomial.polyval(p, 5)
Out[80]: Polynomial([ 5.], [-1.,  1.], [-1.,  1.])
```

The integration and derivation is also done with the built-in functions in the `Polynomial` class as `roots()`, but the function names change to `integ()` and `derive()`:

```
In [81]: p.integ()
Out[81]: Polynomial([  0.    ,   1.    ,  -5.    ,  11.6667, -12.5    ,
4.8  ], [-1.,  1.], [-1.,  1.])
In [82]: p.integ().deriv() == p
Out[82]: True
```

The polynomial package also provides special polynomials such as Chebyshev, Legendre, and Hermite. For more details on these, please refer to `http://docs.scipy.org/doc/numpy-1.10.0/reference/routines.polynomials.classes.html`.

In summary, for most cases `ndarray` and NumPy functions can solve problems related to polynomials. They are also a more preferred way since there is less conversion between types in the program, meaning fewer potential issues. However, when dealing with special polynomials, we still need the polynomial package. We are almost done with the math part. In the next section, we will talk about the application of linear algebra.

Application – regression and curve fitting

Since we are talking about the application of linear algebra, our experience comes from real-world cases. Let's begin with linear regression. So, let's say we are curious about the relationship between the age of a person and his/her sleeping quality. We'll use the data available online from the Great British Sleep Survey 2012 (`https://www.sleepio.com/2012report/`).

There were 20,814 people who took the survey, in an age range from under 20 to over 60 years old, and they evaluated their sleeping quality by scores from 4 to 6.

In this practice, we will just use 100 as our total population and simulate the age and sleeping scores followed the same distribution as the survey results. We want to know whether their age grows, sleep quality (scores) increases or decreases? As you already know, this is a hidden linear regression practice. Once we drew the regression line of the age and sleeping scores, by looking at the slope of the line, the answer will just come up.

But before we talk about which NumPy function we should use and how we use it, let's create the dataset first. From the survey, we know there are 7% of participants under 20, 24% between 21 and 30, 21% between 31 and 40, and 21% over 60. So we first create a group list to represent the number of people in each age group and use `numpy.random.randint()` to simulate the real age among our 100 population, to see the age variable. Now we know the distribution of sleeping scores based on each age group, which we called `scores`: it's a list of [5.5, 5.7, 5.4, 4.9, 4.6, 4.4], the order according to the age group from youngest to the oldest. Here we also use the `np.random.rand()` function with the mean (from the scores list) and the standard variance (all set to 0.01) to simulate the score distribution (of course, if you have a good dataset you want to play with, it would be better to just use the `numpy.genfromtxt()` function we introduced in the previous chapter):

```
In [83]: groups = [7, 24, 21, 19, 17, 12]

In [84]: age = np.concatenate([np.random.randint((ind + 1)*10, (ind +
2)*10, group) for ind, group in enumerate(groups)])

In [85]: age
Out[85]:
array(
[11, 15, 12, 17, 17, 18, 12, 26, 29, 24, 28, 25, 27, 25, 26, 24, 23,  27,
26, 24, 27, 20, 28, 20, 22, 21, 23, 25, 27, 24, 25, 35, 39, 33, 35, 30, 32,
32, 36, 38, 31, 35, 38, 31, 37, 36, 39, 30, 36, 33, 36, 37, 45, 41, 44, 48,
45, 40, 44, 42, 47, 46, 47, 42, 42, 42, 44, 40, 40, 47, 47, 57, 56, 53, 53,
57, 54, 55, 53, 52, 54, 57, 53, 58, 58, 54, 57, 55, 64, 67, 60, 63, 68, 65,
66, 63, 67, 64, 68, 66]
)
In [86]: scores = [5.5, 5.7, 5.4, 4.9, 4.6, 4.4]
In [87]: sim_scores = np.concatenate([.01 * np.random.rand(group) +
scores[ind] for ind, group in enumerate(groups)] )

In [88]: sim_scores
Out[88]:
array([
5.5089,   5.5015,   5.5024,   5.5  ,   5.5033,   5.5019,   5.5012,
5.7068,   5.703 ,   5.702 ,   5.7002,   5.7084,   5.7004,   5.7036,
5.7055,   5.7024,   5.7099,   5.7009,   5.7013,   5.7093,   5.7076,
5.7029,   5.702 ,   5.7067,   5.7007,   5.7004,   5.7  ,   5.7017,
```

```
5.702 ,  5.7031,  5.7087,  5.4079,  5.4082,  5.4083,  5.4025,
5.4008,  5.4069,  5.402 ,  5.4071,  5.4059,  5.4037,  5.4004,
5.4024,  5.4058,  5.403 ,  5.4041,  5.4075,  5.4062,  5.4014,
5.4089,  5.4003,  5.4058,  4.909 ,  4.9062,  4.9097,  4.9014,
4.9097,  4.9023,  4.9   ,  4.9002,  4.903 ,  4.9062,  4.9026,
4.9094,  4.9099,  4.9071,  4.9058,  4.9067,  4.9005,  4.9016,
4.9093,  4.6041,  4.6031,  4.6016,  4.6021,  4.6079,  4.6046,
4.6055,  4.609 ,  4.6052,  4.6005,  4.6017,  4.6091,  4.6073,
4.6029,  4.6012,  4.6062,  4.6098,  4.4014,  4.4043,  4.4013,
4.4091,  4.4087,  4.4087,  4.4027,  4.4017,  4.4067,  4.4003,
4.4021,  4.4061])
```

Now we have the age and sleeping scores and each variable has 100 incidents. Next, we will calculate the regression line: $y = mx + c$, where y represents `sleeping_score`, and x represents `age`. The NumPy function for the regression line is `numpy.linalg.lstsq()` and it takes the coefficient matrix and dependent variable values as inputs. So the first thing we need to do is to pack the variable age into a coefficient matrix, which we call AGE:

```
In [87]: AGE = np.vstack([age, np.ones(len(age))]).T
In [88]: m, c = np.linalg.lstsq(AGE, sim_scores)[0]
In [89]: m
Out[90]: -0.029435313781
In [91]: c
Out[92]: 6.30307651938
```

Now we have the slope m and constant c. Our regression line is $y = -0.0294x + 6.3031$, which shows that, when people grow older, there is a slight decrease in their sleeping scores/quality, as you can see in the following graph:

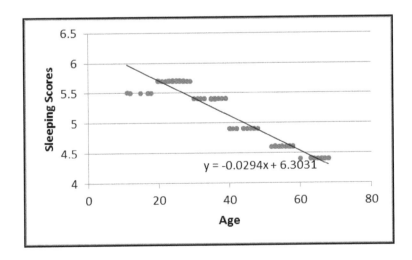

You may think that the regression line equation looks familiar. Remember the first linear equation we solved in the matrix section? Yes, you can also use `numpy.linalg.lstsq()` to solve the $Ax = b$ equation, and actually it will be the fourth solution in this chapter. Try it by yourself; the usage is very similar to when you used `numpy.linalg.solve()`.

However, not every question can simply be answered by drawing a regression line, such as the housing price by year. It's apparently not a linear relation, and is probably a squared or third-degree relation. So how do we solve such a problem? Let's use the statistical data from the House Price Indices (Office for National Statistics, `http://ons.gov.uk/ons/taxonomy/index.html?nscl=House+Price+Indices#tab-data-tables`) and pick the years 2004 to 2013. We have the average house price (in £GBP) adjusted by inflation; we want to know the average price for next year.

Before we go for the solution, let's analyze the question first. Underlying the question is a polynomial curve fitting problem; we want to find the best-fit polynomial for our questions, but which NumPy function should we choose for it? But before doing that, let's create two variables: the price by each year, `price`, and the year of the house, `year`:

```
In [93]: year = np.arange(1,11)
In [94]: price = np.array([129000, 133000, 138000, 144000, 142000, 141000,
150000, 135000, 134000, 139000]).
In [95]: year
Out[95]: array([ 1,  2,  3,  4,  5,  6,  7,  8,  9, 10])
```

Now we have the year and price data, let's assume their relation is squared. Our goal is to find the polynomial: $y = ax2 + bx + c$ to represent the relations (a typical least-squares approach). y represents `price` at x year. Here we will use `numpy.polyfit()` to help us find the coefficients for this polynomial:

```
In [97]: a, b, c = np.polyfit(year, price, 2)
In [98]: a
Out[98]: -549.242424242
In [99]: b
Out[99]: 6641.66666667
In [100]: c
Out[100]: 123116.666667
In [101]: a*11**2 + b*11 + c
Out[101]: 129716.66666666642
```

We have all the coefficients for the polynomial from `numpy.polyfit()`, which takes three input parameters: the first one stands for the independent variable: `year`; the second one is the dependent variable: `price`; and the last one is the degree of the polynomial, which in this case is 2. Now we just need to use `year = 11` (11 years from 2004), then the estimated price can be calculated. You can see the result in the following graph:

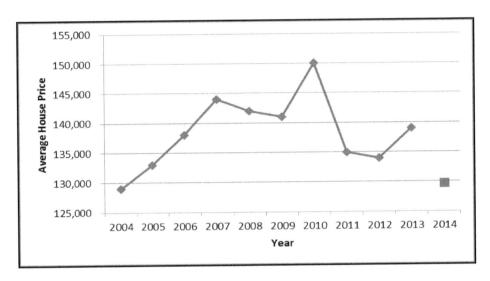

There are many applications from linear algebra that NumPy can achieve such as interpolation and extrapolation, but we can't cover them all in this chapter. We hope this chapter is a good start for you to use NumPy to solve linear or polynomial problems.

Summary

In this chapter, we covered the matrix class and polynomial class for linear algebra. We looked at the advanced functions provided by both classes, and also saw the performance advantage given by `ndarray` when doing the basic transpose. Also we introduced the `numpy.linalg` class, which provides many functions to deal with linear or polynomial computations with `ndarray`.

We did lots of math in this chapter, but we also found out how to use NumPy to help us answer some real-world questions.

In next chapter, we will get to know Fourier transformation and its application within NumPy.

6
Fourier Analysis in NumPy

Fourier analysis is commonly used, among other things, for digital signal processing. This is thanks to it being so powerful in separating its input signals (time domain) into components that contribute at discrete frequencies (frequency domain). Another fast algorithm to compute **Discrete Fourier transform** (**DFT**) was developed, which is well known as **Fast Fourier transform** (**FFT**), and it provides more possibilities for analysis and its applications. NumPy, as it targets numeric computing, also supports FFT. Let's try to use NumPy to apply some Fourier analysis on applications! Note, no familiarity with signal processing or Fourier methods is assumed in this chapter.

The topics that will be covered in this chapter are:

- The basics of Fourier analysis
- One and two-dimensional Fourier transformations
- Spectral density estimation
- Time frequency analysis

Before we start

As we all know, Fourier analysis expresses a function as a sum of periodic components (a combination of sine and cosine functions) and these components are able to recover the original function. It has great applications in digital signal processing such as filtering, interpolation, and more, so we don't want to talk about Fourier analysis in NumPy without giving details of any application we can use it for. For this, we need a module to visualize it.

Matplotlib is the module we are going to use in this chapter for visualization. Please download and install it from the official website: `http://matplotlib.org/downloads.html`. Or if you are using Scientific Python distributions such as Anaconda, then matplotlib should already be included.

We are going to write a simple display function called `show()` to help us with the practice examples in this chapter. The function output will be as shown in the following graph:

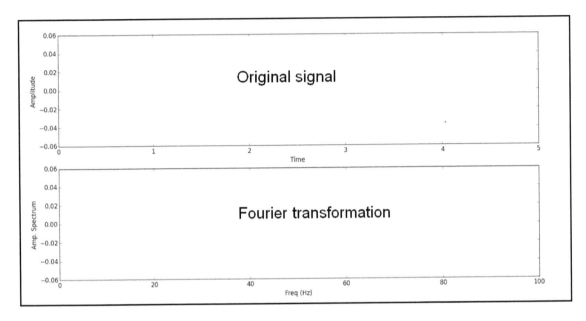

The upper plot area shows the original functions (signal), and the lower plot shows the Fourier transformation. Please type the following code into your IPython command prompt or save it to a `.py` file and load it to the prompt:

```
#### The Plotting Functions ####import matplotlib.pyplot as plt
import numpy as np
def show(ori_func, ft, sampling_period = 5):
    n = len(ori_func)
    interval = sampling_period / n
    plt.subplot(2, 1, 1)
    plt.plot(np.arange(0, sampling_period, interval), ori_func, 'black')
    plt.xlabel('Time'), plt.ylabel('Amplitude')
    plt.subplot(2,1,2)
    frequency = np.arange(n / 2) / (n * interval)
    nfft = abs(ft[range(int(n / 2))] / n )
    plt.plot(frequency, nfft, 'red')
    plt.xlabel('Freq (Hz)'), plt.ylabel('Amp. Spectrum')
    plt.show()
```

This is a display function called `show()`, which has two input parameters: the first one is the original signal function (`ori_func`) and the second one is its Fourier transform (`ft`). This method will use the `matplotlib.pyplot` module to create two line charts: the original signal at the top with black lines, where the *x* axis represents the time intervals (we set the default signal sampling period to be five seconds for our all examples) and the *y* axis represents the amplitude of the signal. The lower part of the chart is its Fourier transform with a red line, where the *x* axis represents the frequency and the *y* axis represents the amplitude spectrum.

In the next section, we will simply go through different types of signal waves and use the `numpy.fft` module to compute the Fourier transform. Then we call the `show()` function to provide a visual comparison between them.

Signal processing

In this section, we are going to use NumPy functions to simulate several signal functions and translate them to Fourier transforms. We will focus on using `numpy.fft` and its related functions. We hope after this section that you will get some sense of using a Fourier transformation in NumPy. The theory part will be covered in the next section.

The first example we are going to use is our heartbeat signal, which is a series of sine waves. The frequency is 60 beats per minutes (1 Hz), and our sampling period is 5 seconds long, with a sampling interval of 0.005 seconds. Let's create the sine wave first:

```
In [1]: time = np.arange(0, 5, .005)
In [2]: x = np.sin(2 * np.pi * 1 * time)
In [3]: y = np.fft.fft(x)
In [4]: show(x, y)
```

In this example, we first created the sampling time interval and saved it to an ndarray called time. And we passed the time array times 2π and its frequency 1 Hz to the numpy.sin() method to create the sine wave (x). Then applied the Fourier transform to x and saved it to y. Finally, we used our predefined method show() for visual comparison with the sine wave and its normalized Fourier transform, as you can see in the following graph:

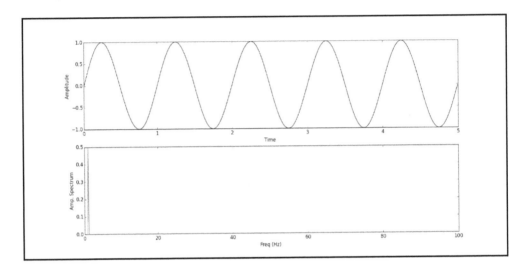

The upper green line represents the heartbeat wave; since we use 1 Hz for 5 seconds, we obtained 5 continuous sine waves. One thing to note here is that our sampling interval is 0.005 seconds, which means we use 200 points (1/0.005) to simulate one wave, so it looks relatively smooth. If we increase our sampling interval (reducing the number of points for each wave), we will obtain a more intense sine wave. The lower part of the chart is the absolute value of the normalized Fourier transform based on the frequencies (the so-called spectrum). We can see that there is a high point at 1 Hz, which matches our original wave frequency.

Next, we are going to try computing multi-frequency sine waves to their Fourier transforms. After this, we may have a clearer picture of a Fourier transform. The following code shows you how to do this:

```
In [8]: x2 = np.sin(2 * np.pi * 20 * time)
In [9]: x3 = np.sin(2 * np.pi * 60 * time)
In [10]: x += x2 + x3
In [11]: y = np.fft.fft(x)
In [12]: show(x, y)
```

First, we created two more sine waves with a different frequency, x2 with a frequency of 20 Hz, and x3 with 60 Hz, and we added them to the original 1Hz sine waves x. Then we passed the modified x to the Fourier transform and plotted the graph using the predefined `show()`. You can see this in the following graph:

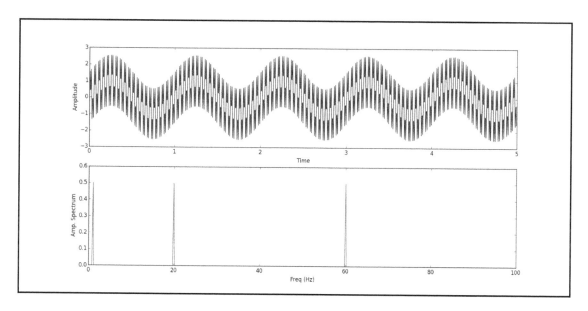

In the upper green line chart, we can see that the sine waves are combined with different frequencies, but it is really difficult to distinguish them. However, after computing the Fourier transform, and converting them to the frequency domain, we can see clearly in the lower red line chart that three high points are identified, which are 1 Hz, 20 Hz, and 60 Hz. This matches up with our original sine wave's frequency.

From these two examples, you must be able to get some sense of the Fourier transform. Next we are going to demonstrate three more signal processings: one for square signals, one for pulses, and the other for random signals.

First we created square wave signals using `numpy.zeros()` with the same time intervals (`time`). We want the square wave frequency to be 10 Hz and the amplitude to be 1, so we set every 20th time interval (*200 / 10*) to be a value of one to simulate the wave and pass it to the Fourier transform, as you can see in the following code block:

```
In [13]: x = np.zeros(len(time))
In [14]: x[::20] = 1
In [15]: y = np.fft.fft(x)
In [16]: show(x, y)
```

This code generates the following graph:

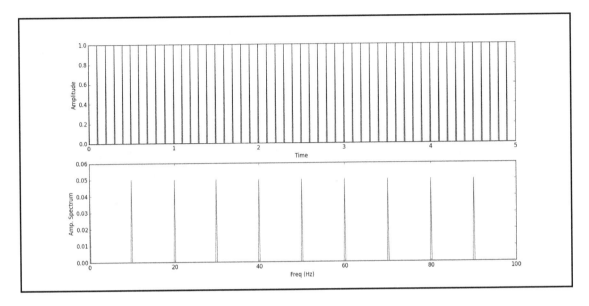

From the upper green line chart, we can see 50 continuous square waves in 5 seconds (10 Hz), but when we computed its Fourier transform we obtained several red high points in the spectrum instead of just one at 10 Hz. You may wonder whether square waves are also periodic functions, but why is the Fourier transform so different from the sine waves? Remember that the Fourier transform converts the time domain to the frequency domain but, underneath the hood, there are series of sine and cosine functions to decompose the original function. We can still see the red high points are regularly spaced, where the space is 10 Hz apart.

Next, we are going to generate a one-pulse signal, that doesn't have any frequency, and we are going to compute its Fourier transform. Compare this with the previous square waves, and you may have a better sense of the Fourier transform:

```
In [17]: x = np.zeros(len(time))
In [18]: x[380:400] = np.arange(0, 1, .05)
In [19]: x[400:420] = np.arange(1, 0, -.05)
In [20]: y = np.fft.fft(x)
In [21]: show(x, y)
```

First we created an all-zero `ndarray` the same size as the time variable, and then we generated the one-pulse signal, which occurred at 2 seconds (the 400th element of the x array). We occupied 40 elements around 2 seconds to simulate the pulse: 20 increasing from 0 to 1, and the other half decreasing from 1 back to 0. We passed the one-pulse signal to the Fourier transform and used `show()` for visual comparison.

The upper green line chart in the following graph is the one-pulse signal we simulated, and the lower red line chart is its Fourier transform. We can see the highest point in the lower chart occurred in frequency equal to 0, which makes perfect sense since our simulated signal didn't have any frequency. But, after zero-frequency, we can still see a couple of high points at different frequencies, which came from the transformation processes.

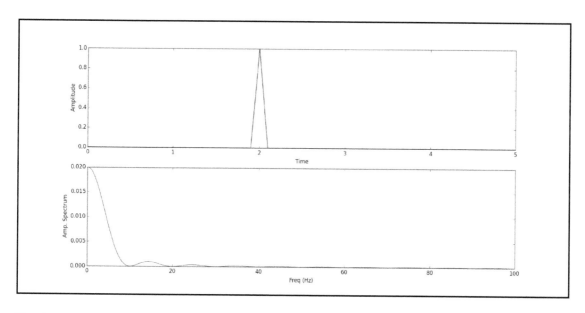

The last example in this section is random signal processing. As in the previous example, we also use 5 seconds as our total sampling period with 100 random signals, which doesn't have any fixed frequency associated with it. And we pass the random signals to the Fourier transform to obtain its frequency domain. The code block is as follows:

```
In [22]: x = np.random.random(100)
In [23]: y = np.fft.fft(x)
In [24]: show(x, y)
```

The following is the graph generated by the code:

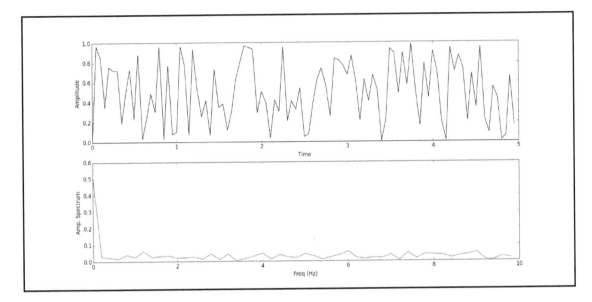

After going through these examples, we know how to use the Fourier transform in NumPy- simply call `numpy.fft.fft()`-and we gained some sense of what the Fourier transform looks like. In the next section, we will focus on the theory part.

Fourier analysis

There are many ways to define the DFT; however, in a NumPy implementation, the DFT is defined as the following equation:

$$A_k = \sum_{m=0}^{n-1} a_m \exp\left\{-2\pi i\frac{mk}{n}\right\} \quad k = 0,1,\ldots,n-1$$

A_k represents the discrete Fourier transform and a_m represents the original function. The transformation from a_m->A_k is a translation from the configuration space to the frequency space. Let's calculate this equation manually to get a better understanding of the transformation process. We will use a random signal with 500 values:

```
In [25]: x = np.random.random(500)
In [26]: n = len(x)
In [27]: m = np.arange(n)
In [28]: k = m.reshape((n, 1))
In [29]: M = np.exp(-2j * np.pi * k * m / n)
In [30]: y = np.dot(M, x)
```

In this code block, x is our simulated random signal, which contain 500 values and corresponds to a_m in the equation. Based on the size of x, we calculate the sum product of:

$$\exp\left\{-2\pi i\,\frac{mk}{n}\right\}$$

We then save it to M. The final step is to use the matrix multiplication between M and x to generate DFT and save it to y.

Let's verify our result by comparing it with the built-in numpy.fft:

```
In [31]: np.allclose(y, np.fft.fft(x))
Out[31]: True
```

As we expected, the manually computed DFT is identical to the NumPy built-in module. Of course, numpy.fft is just like any other built-in modules in NumPy-it's been optimized and the FFT algorithm has been applied. Let's compare the performance between our manual DFT and numpy.fft:

```
In [32]: %timeit np.dot(np.exp(-2j * np.pi * np.arange(n).reshape((n, 1)) *
np.arange(n) / n), x)
10 loops, best of 3: 18.5 ms per loop
In [33]: %timeit np.fft.fft(x)
100000 loops, best of 3: 10.9 µs per loop
```

First, we put this equation implementation code on one line in order to measure the execution time. We can see a huge performance difference between them. Underneath the hood, NumPy uses the FFTPACK library to perform the Fourier transform, which is a very stable library both in performance and accuracy.

If you still feel that FFTPACK is not fast enough, there is a FFTW library that normally performs better than FFTPACK, but the speed-up from FFTPACK to FFTW would not be nearly as dramatic.

Next, we are going to compute the inverse DFT. The iDFT maps the frequency series back to the original time series, which is defined in the following equation:

$$a_m = \frac{1}{n} \sum_{k=0}^{n-1} A_k \exp\left\{2\pi i \frac{mk}{n}\right\} \qquad m = 0, 1, \ldots, n-1$$

We can see the inverse equation differs from the DFT equation by the sign of the exponential argument and the normalization by *1/n*. Let's do the manual calculation again. We can re-use the m, k, and n variables from the previous code and just re-compute M due to the sign change of the exponential argument:

```
In [34]: M2 = np.exp(2j * np.pi * k * m / n)
In [35]: x2 = np.dot(y, M2) / n
```

Again, let's verify the computed inverse DFT result x2 with our original random signal x. The two ndarray should be identical:

```
In [36]: np.allclose(x, x2)
Out[36]: True
```

Of course, the numpy.fft module also support inverse DFT-simply call numpy.fft.ifft() to perform the computation, as you can see in the following example:

```
In [37]: np.allclose(x, np.fft.ifft(y))
Out[37]: True
```

You may notice that, in the previous examples, we always use a one-dimensional array as our input signals. Does that mean that numpy.fft only handles one-dimensional data? Of course not; numpy.fft can also process two- or multi-dimensional data. Before we get to this part, we'd like to talk about the order of returned FFT arrays and a shift method in numpy.fft.

Let's create a simple signal array with 10 random integers, and compute its Fourier transform:

```
In [38]: a = np.random.randint(10, size = 10)
In [39]: a
Out[39]: array([7, 4, 9, 9, 6, 9, 2, 6, 8, 3])
In [40]: a.mean()
Out[40]: 6.2999999999999998
In [41]: A = np.fft.fft(a)
In [42]: A
Out[42]:
array([ 63.00000000 +0.00000000e+00j,
        -2.19098301 -6.74315233e+00j,
        -5.25328890 +4.02874005e+00j,
        -3.30901699 -2.40414157e+00j,
        13.75328890 -1.38757276e-01j,
         1.00000000 -2.44249065e-15j,
        13.75328890 +1.38757276e-01j,
        -3.30901699 +2.40414157e+00j,
        -5.25328890 -4.02874005e+00j,
        -2.19098301 +6.74315233e+00j])
In [43]: A[0] / 10
Out[43]: (6.2999999999999998+0j)
In [44]: A[int(10 / 2)]
Out[44]: (1-2.4424906541753444e-15j)
```

In this example, a is our original random signal and A is a's Fourier transform. When we call numpy.fft.fft(a), the resulting ndarray follows the "standard" order in which the first value A[0] contains the zero-frequency term (the mean of the signal). When we do the normalization, which is dividing it by the length of the original signal array (A[0] / 10), we get the same value as when we calculated the mean of the signal array (a.mean()).

Then A[1:n/2] contains the positive-frequency terms and A[n/2 + 1: n] contains the negative-frequency terms. When the inputs are even numbers as in our example, A[n/2] represents both positive and negative. If you want to shift the zero-frequency component to the center of the spectrum, we can use the numpy.fft.fftshift() routine. See the following example:

```
In [45]: np.fft.fftshift(A)
Out[45]:
array([   1.00000000 -2.44249065e-15j,
         13.75328890 +1.38757276e-01j,
         -3.30901699 +2.40414157e+00j,
         -5.25328890 -4.02874005e+00j,
         -2.19098301 +6.74315233e+00j,
         63.00000000 +0.00000000e+00j,
```

```
        -2.19098301 -6.74315233e+00j,
     -5.25328890 +4.02874005e+00j,
        -3.30901699 -2.40414157e+00j,
     13.75328890 -1.38757276e-01j])
```

From this example, you can see that `numpy.fft.fftshift()` swaps half-spaces in the array, so the zero-frequency components are shifted to the middle. `numpy.fft.ifftshift` is the inverse function, shifting the order back to "standard".

Now, we are going to talk multi-dimensional DFT; let's start with two dimensions. You may see that the following equation is very similar to a one-dimensional DFT, and the second dimension is extended in the obvious way. The idea for multi-dimensional DFT is the same, and so does the inverses in higher dimensions. You may also try to modify the previous codes to calculate the one-dimensional DFT to two or multi-dimensional DFT to better understand the processes. But now we are simply going to demonstrate how to use `numpy.fft` for two-dimensional and multi-dimensional Fourier transforms:

$$A_{kl} = \sum_{m=0}^{M-1} \sum_{n=0}^{N-1} a_{mn} \exp\left\{-2\pi i \left(\frac{mk}{M} + \frac{nl}{N}\right)\right\} \quad k = 0,1,\ldots,M-1; l = 0,1,\ldots,N-1$$

```
In [46]: x = np.random.random(24)
In [47]: x.shape = 2,12
In [48]: y2 = np.fft.fft2(x)
In [49]: x.shape = 1,2,12
In [50]: y3 = np.fft.fftn(x, axes = (1, 2))
```

From these examples, you can see that we call `numpy.fft.fft2()` for a two-dimensional Fourier transform, and `numpy.fft.fftn()` for multi-dimensional. The axes parameter is optional; it indicates the axes over which to compute the FFT. For two-dimensional, if the axes are not specified, it uses the last two axes; while for multi-dimensional, the module uses all the axes. In the previous example, we applied the last two axes only, so the Fourier transform result will be identical to the two-dimensional one. Let's check it out:

```
In [51]: np.allclose(y2, y3)
Out[51]: True
```

Fourier transform application

In the previous sections, you learned how to use `numpy.fft` for a one and multi-dimensional `ndarray`, and saw the implementation details underneath the hood. Now it's time for some applications. In this section, we are going to use the Fourier transform to do some image processing. We will analyze the spectrum, and then we will interpolate the image to enlarge it to twice the size. First, let's download the exercise image from the Packt Publishing website blog post: `https://www.packtpub.com/books/content/python-data-scientists`. Save the image to your local directory as `scientist.png`.

This is a RGB image, which means that, when we convert it to an `ndarray`, it will be three-dimensional. To simplify the exercise, we use the image module in `matplotlib` to read in the image and convert it to grayscale:

```
In [52]: from matplotlib import image
In [53]: img = image.imread('./scientist.png')
In [54]: gray_img = np.dot(img[:,:,:3], [.21, .72, .07])
In [55]: gray_img.shape
Out[55]: (317L, 661L)
In [56]: plt.imshow(gray_img, cmap = plt.get_cmap('gray'))
Out[56]: <matplotlib.image.AxesImage at 0xa6165c0>
In [57]: plt.show()
```

You will get the following image as the result:

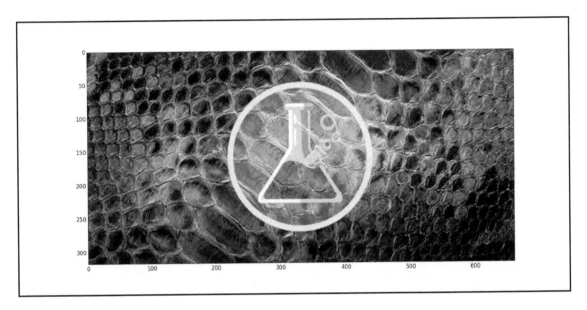

The pre-processing part is done. We read the image into a three-dimensional `ndarray` (img) and applied the luminosity formula to convert the RGB image to grayscale using *0.21R + 0.72G + 0.07B*. We used the `pyplot` module in `matplotlib` to show the grayscale image. Here we didn't apply any axis label in the plot, but we can see from the axis scale that `ndarraygray_img` represents a 317 x 661 pixel image.

Next, we are going to do the Fourier transform and show the spectrum:

```
In [58]: fft = np.fft.fft2(gray_img)
In [59]: amp_spectrum = np.abs(fft)
In [60]: plt.imshow(np.log(amp_spectrum))
Out[60]: <matplotlib.image.AxesImage at 0xcdeff60>
In [61]: plt.show()
```

This code will give the following output:

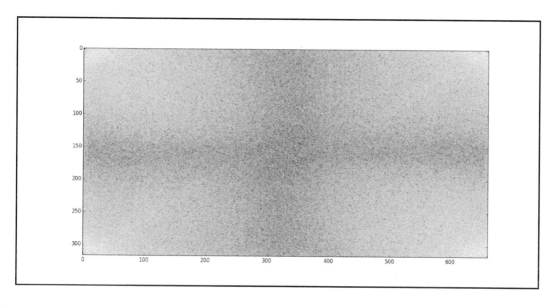

First, we use a two-dimensional Fourier transform for `gray_img`, and plot the amplitude spectrum using a log-scale color map. We can see that the corners are different due to the zero-frequency component. Remember, when we use `numpy.fft.fft2()`, the order follows the *standard* order, and we want to place the zero-frequency component to the center. So let's use the shift routine:

```
In [62]: fft_shift = np.fft.fftshift(fft)
In [63]: plt.imshow(np.log(np.abs(fft_shift)))
Out[63]: <matplotlib.image.AxesImage at 0xd201dd8>
In [64]: plt.show()
```

This changes the image to:

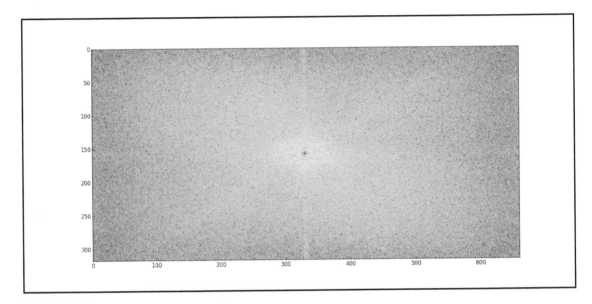

We can now see that the zero-frequency component is in the center. Let's go to the last step of this exercise: interpolating the image to enlarge the size. The techniques we are using here are very simple; we interpolate zero-frequency into the `fft_shift` array and make it twice the size. Then we inverse `fft_shift` to the standard order and do another inverse transform back to the original domain:

```
In [65]: m, n = fft_shift.shape
In [66]: b = np.zeros((int(m / 2), n))
In [67]: c = np.zeros((2 * m - 1, int(n / 2)))
In [68]: fft_shift = np.concatenate((b, fft_shift, b), axis = 0)
In [69]: fft_shift = np.concatenate((c, fft_shift, c), axis = 1)
In [70]: ifft = np.fft.ifft2(np.fft.ifftshift(fft_shift))
In [71]: ifft.shape
Out[71]: (633L, 1321L)
In [72]: ifft = np.real(ifft)
In [73]: plt.imshow(ifft, cmap = plt.get_cmap('gray'))
Out[73]: <matplotlib.image.AxesImage at 0xf9a0f98>
In [74]: plt.show()
```

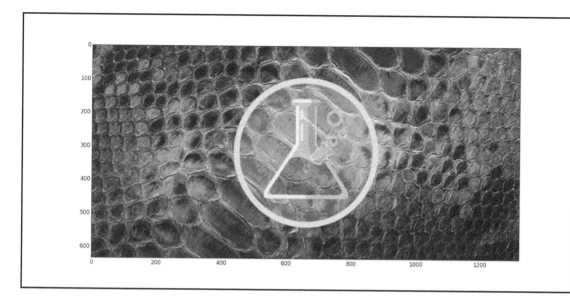

In the previous code block, we first retrieved the shape of our `fft_shift` array (the same size as `gray_img`). Then we created two zero `ndarrays` and padded them to the `fft_shift` array in four directions to enlarge it. So when we inverse the modified `fft_shift` array back to the standard order, the zero-frequency will be perfectly in the middle. And when we do the inverse transformation, you can see that the shape has been doubled. In order to let the `pyplot` module plot the new array, we need to convert the array to real numbers. After plotting the new array, we can see that the axis scales are double the size. And we barely lose any details or get any image blur as a result of it. The image has been interpolated using the Fourier transformation.

Summary

In this chapter, we covered the usage of one and multi-dimensional Fourier transformations and how they are applied in signal processing. You now understand the implementation of the discrete Fourier transform in NumPy, and we did a performance comparison between our manual implemented script with NumPy built-in modules.

We also accomplished a real-world application of image interpolation, and we got a plus one for knowing some basics of the `matplotlib` packages.

In the next chapter, we will see how to distribute our code using the `numpy.distutils()` submodules.

7
Building and Distributing NumPy Code

In a real-world scenario, you will be writing an application with the intentions of distributing it to the World or reusing it on various other computers. For this purpose, you would like your application to be packed in a standard way so that everyone in the community understands and follows. As you will have noticed by now, Python users mainly use a package manager called `pip` to automate the installation of modules created by other programmers. Python has a packaging platform called **PyPI** (**Python Package Index**), which is an official central repository for more than 50,000 Python packages. Once the package is registered in PyPi aka *Cheese Shop*, other users across the world can install it after configuring it with package management systems such as `pip`. Python comes with a number of solutions to help you to build your code ready for distribution to the *Cheese Shop* and, in this chapter, we will focus on two such tools, `setuptools` and `Distutils`. Apart from these two tools, we will be looking into a specific module provided by NumPy called `numpy.distutils`. This module makes the process of building and distributing NumPy-specific code easier for the programmers. This module also provides added functionalities such as methods for compiling Fortran code, calling `f2py`, and more. In this chapter, we will be going through the following steps to learn the packaging workflow:

- We will build a small but working setup
- We will explain the steps to integrate NumPy modules into your setup
- We will explain how to register and distribute your application over the Internet

Introducing Distutils and setuptools

Before we begin, first let us understand what these tools are and why we prefer one over another. Distutils is a framework that comes by default with Python, and setuptools builds over the standard Distutils to provide enhanced functionalities and features. In a real-world scenario, you will never use Distutils. The only case where you might want to use Distutils alone is where setuptools is unavailable. (A good setup script should check for the availability of setuptools before proceeding.) In most cases, users will be better off installing setuptools as most packages nowadays are built over them. We will be using setuptools for building Cython code in the following chapters; hence, for our purpose, we will be installing setuptools now and using it extensively from now on.

Next let us start by installing the required tools to build our first dummy (but working) installer. After we have got our installer working, we will dive into more functionalities covering NumPy in a real-world script for the pandas module. We will study the checks made in the scripts to make it more robust and how we provide more information in the event of failures.

Preparing the tools

To install setuptools on your system, you need to first download ez_setup.py on your system from https://pypi.python.org/pypi/setuptools and then execute this from your command prompt as follows:

```
$ python ez_setup.py
```

To test the installation of setuptools, open the Python shell and type the following:

```
> import setuptools
```

If the preceding import does not give any error, then we have successfully installed setuptools.

Building the first working distribution

All of the tools we mentioned previously (`setuptools`, `Distutils` and `numpy.distutils`) are centered around the function setup. To get an understanding of most packaging requirements, we will look into a simple setup function and then study a full-fledged installer. To create a basic installer, we need to call the setup function with metadata about the package. Let's call our first package `py_hello`, which has just one function `greeter`, and just prints a message when called. The package can be downloaded from the Bitbucket repository at `https://bitbucket.org/tdatta/books/src/af376df 081ef/python/simple_setup/?at=master` The project directory structure for the project looks like the following:

```
py_hello
├── README
├── MANIFEST.in
├── setup.py
├── bin
│   └── greeter.bat
└── greeter
    ├── __init__.py
    ├── greeter.py
```

Let's look at some standard files here:

- `README`-This file is used to store information about your project. This file is not required by the system and you will still get your installer build without it, but it is a good practice to keep it here.
- `MANIFEST.in`-This is a text file that is used by `Distutils` to collect all the files in your project. It is very important, and only the files listed here go into the final installer `tar` archive. In addition to specifying files that should go in the final installer, `manifest` can be used to exclude certain files from the project directory. The `manifest` file is mandatory; if it is not present, you will get an error while using `setup.py`. If you have an `svn` setup, then you can use the `sdist` command to automatically include files by parsing your `.svn` file and building the `manifest.in` file.
- `__init__.py`-This file is important for Python to recognize the directory as a module. You may leave it empty after creating it.

To create an installer for this setup, we have `setup.py` in root, which uses the `setup` function from `setuptools`:

```
from setuptools import setup
import os
description = open(os.path.join(os.path.dirname(__file__), 'README'),
'r').read()
setup(
    name = "py_hello",
    packages = ["greeter"],
    scripts = ["bin/greeter.bat"],
    include_package_data = True,
    package_data = {
        "py_hello":[]
        },
    version = "0.1.0",
    description = "Simple Application",
    author = "packt",
    author_email = "packt@packt.com",
    url = "https://bitbucket.org/tdatta/book/py_hello",
    download_url =
"https://bitbucket.org/tdatta/book/py_hello/zipball/master",
    keywords = ["tanmay", "example_seutp", "packt"  "app"],
    install_requires=[
        "setup >= 0.1"],
    license='LICENSE',
    classifiers = [
        "Programming Language :: Python",
        "Development Status :: release 0.1",
        "Intended Audience ::  new users",
        "License :: Public",
        "Operating System :: POSIX :: Linux",
        "Topic :: Demo",
        ],
    long_description = description
    )
```

The following are the options used in the setup:

- `name`-This is the name of the installation TAR archive.
- `packages`-This is a list naming the packages you want to include.
- `scripts`-This is a list of script(s) to be installed into standard locations such as `/usr/bin`. In this particular case, there is just an echo script. The intention for this is to just show readers how you can ship scripts with your package.
- `package_data`-This is a dictionary with the key (package) associated to the list of files.

- `version`: -This is the version of your project. This gets appended to the end of your installer's name.
- `long_description`-This will be turned into HTML when displayed at the PyPI website. It should contain information about what your project is intending to provide. You can directly write it in the script; however, the best practice is to maintain the README file and read the description from there.
- `install_required`-This is a list that is used to add dependencies for your installation. You will add the name and version of third-party modules used within your code. Note the convention followed to specify the version here.
- `classifiers`-This will be checked when you upload the package on the PyPI website. One should choose from the options given at the following website: `https://pypi.python.org/pypi?:action=list_classifiers`

Running `setup.py` with the **build** option now should give you no error and produce a folder with the `.egg-info` suffix. At this point, you can run `setup.py` with the **sdist** option and create a package that is ready to be shared with the World.

You should see the final message as **Creating tar archive** as shown below:

```
                       /py_hello $ python setup.py sdist
running sdist
running egg_info
writing requirements to py_hello.egg-info/requires.txt
writing py_hello.egg-info/PKG-INFO
writing top-level names to py_hello.egg-info/top_level.txt
writing dependency_links to py_hello.egg-info/dependency_links.txt
reading manifest file 'py_hello.egg-info/SOURCES.txt'
reading manifest template 'MANIFEST.in'
warning: no files found matching 'README.txt'
warning: no files found matching '*.py' under directory '*.txt'
writing manifest file 'py_hello.egg-info/SOURCES.txt'
running check
creating py_hello-0.1.0
creating py_hello-0.1.0/bin
creating py_hello-0.1.0/greeter
creating py_hello-0.1.0/py_hello.egg-info
making hard links in py_hello-0.1.0...
hard linking MANIFEST.in -> py_hello-0.1.0
hard linking README -> py_hello-0.1.0
hard linking setup.py -> py_hello-0.1.0
hard linking bin/greeter.bat -> py_hello-0.1.0/bin
hard linking greeter/__init__.py -> py_hello-0.1.0/greeter
hard linking greeter/greeter.py -> py_hello-0.1.0/greeter
hard linking py_hello.egg-info/PKG-INFO -> py_hello-0.1.0/py_hello.egg-info
hard linking py_hello.egg-info/SOURCES.txt -> py_hello-0.1.0/py_hello.egg-info
hard linking py_hello.egg-info/dependency_links.txt -> py_hello-0.1.0/py_hello.e
gg-info
hard linking py_hello.egg-info/requires.txt -> py_hello-0.1.0/py_hello.egg-info
hard linking py_hello.egg-info/top_level.txt -> py_hello-0.1.0/py_hello.egg-info
Writing py_hello-0.1.0/setup.cfg
Creating tar archive
```

To test the package, you can install it on your local machine as follows:

```
python setup.py install
```

And check it as shown in the following:

```
                         py_hello $ python
Python 2.7.6 (default, Jun 22 2015, 17:58:13)
[GCC 4.8.2] on linux2
Type "help", "copyright", "credits" or "license" for more information.
>>> import greeter.greeter
>>> import greeter.greeter as g
>>> g.greet()
Hi tanmay, you are awesome
>>>
```

At this moment, write greeter on your cmd/bash prompt and you will see a message saying does nothing. This echo message is coming from greeter.bat, which we have placed in the scripts key in the setup file.

The next section can be added to this skeleton setup.py to include NumPy-specific features.

Adding NumPy and non-Python source code

Next we will study some NumPy-specific code and understand how to improve the error-handling capabilities of the setup; in general, we will explore some good programming practices. We will also show how to add non-Python source (c, fortran or f2py) into your installer. The following analysis shows part of the full code that you can find on the accompanying code files or at https://bitbucket.org/tdatta/books/:

```
if sys.version_info[0] < 3:
    import __builtin__ as builtins
else:
    import builtins


. . . . .
. . . . .
. . . . .
***For full sample look for setup.py file with the accompanying CD***
. . . . .
. . . . .


#define a function to import numpy if available and return true else false
```

```
def is_numpy_installed():
    try:
        import numpy
    except ImportError:
        return False
    return True
# next we will import setuptools feature here
# We need to do this here because setuptools will "Monkey patch" the setup
function
#
SETUPTOOLS_COMMANDS = set([
    'develop', 'release', 'bdist_egg','bdist_rpm',
    'bdist_wininst', 'install_egg_info', 'build_sphinx',
    'easy_install', 'upload', 'bdist_wheel',
    '--single-version-externally-managed',
])

if SETUPTOOLS_COMMANDS.intersection(sys.argv):
    import setuptools
    extra_setuptools_args = dict(
        zip_safe-False # Custom clean command to remove build artifacts

# The main function where we link everything

def setup_package():

    # check NumPy and raise excpetions
    if is_numpy_installed() is False:
        raise ImportError("Numerical Python (NumPy) is not installed. The
package requires it be installed. Installation instruction available at the
NumPy website")

    from numpy.distutils.core import setup, Extension

    # add extension from Fortran
    ext1 = Extension(name = "firstExt",
                    sources = ['firstExt.f'])
    ext2  = Extension(name = "convolutedExt",
                        sources = ['convolutedExt.pyf, stc2.f'],
                        include_dir = ['paths to include'],
                        extra_objects = "staticlib.a")
    metadata = dict(name = "yourPackage",
                    description="short desc",
                    license = "licence info here",
                    ext_modules = [ext1, ext2]
                    ..
                    # metadata as we set previously
                    ..
```

```
                    **extra_setuptools_args
        )


    setup(**metadata)



if __name__ == "__main__":
    setup_package()
```

The preceding script is stripped from a full working setup to focus on some aspects that you will find in almost all the setup scripts. These tasks ensure that you have done enough error handling and your script does not fail without explaining/hinting what to do next:

1. Check if NumPy is installed. The pattern followed here to ensure that NumPy is installed is a standard pattern that you can use for all the modules that you are planning to use and are required for your setup. To perform this task, we first build a function `is_numpy_installed` that tries to import `numpy` and returns a Boolean value. You will likely create similar functions for all the external packages that your setup file may be using. Advanced users may explore Python decorators to handle this in a more elegant way. If this function returns a false value, the installer should output a warning/info in case it can't finish without this package.

2. Add `Extensions` to the setup file.

3. The `Extension` class is the object that enables us to add non-Python code to our installer. The `sources` argument may contain a list of Fortran source files. However, the list sources may contain at the most one `f2py` signature file, and then the name of an Extension module must match with the `<module>` used in the signature file. The `f2py` signature file must contain exactly one Python module block, otherwise your installer will fail to build. You may decide not to add the signature files in the `sources` argument. In that case, `f2py` will scan for Fortran source files for routine signatures to construct the wrappers to Fortran codes. Additional options for the `f2py` process can be given using the `Extension` class argument `f2py_options`. These options are not in the scope of this book, and most readers will not be using them. For more details, users may refer to the extension class in the `api` document for `numpy.distutils`.

The setup file can be tested as follows:

```
$ python <setup.py file> build_src build_ext --help
```

The `build_src` argument here is used to construct Fortran wrapper extension modules. It is assumed here that the user has compilers for C/C++ and Fortran installed on his machine.

Testing your package

It is very important that the package you are building should work/install without any problem on a user's computer. Hence, you should spend time testing the package. The general idea behind testing installation is to create a virtualenv and try to install the package or use another system altogether. Any error encountered at this stage should be removed and the author should try to make sure that the exceptions are easier to follow. Exceptions should also try to provide the solution. Common mistakes at this stage would be:

- Assumptions about preinstalled modules and libraries.
- Developers may forget to include dependencies in the setup file. This mistake will be caught if you use a new virtualenv to test the installer.
- Permissions and elevated rights requirements.
- Some users may have read-only access to the computer. This could be easily overlooked as most developers do not have this case in their own machines. This problem should not occur if the provider of the package is following the right approach toward selecting the directories for writing. It is generally a good practice to check for this scenario by testing your scripts using a user without admin access.

Distributing your application

Once all the development for your module/application is complete and you are ready with your complete working application and setup file, the next task will be to share your hardwork with the World to benefit others. The steps to release it to the world by using PyPI are quite straightforward. The first thing you need to do as an author of a package is to register yourself. You can do it directly from the command line as follows:

```
$ python setup.py register
running register
running egg_info
. . . .
. . . .
We need to know who you are, so please choose either:
 1. use your existing login,
 2. register as a new user,
```

```
     3. have the server generate a new password for you (and email it to
you), or
     4. quit
   Your selection [default 1]:
```

 This process will fail if you do not have proper metadata information of any file missing in your `setup.py`. Make sure you have `setup.py` working first.

Finally, you can upload your distribution on PyPI by doing the following:

```
$ python setup.py sdist upload
```

Hopefully, if you typed everything correctly, your application will be packaged and available on PyPI for the World to use.

Summary

In this chapter, we introduced the tools used for packaging and distributing applications. We first looked at a simpler `setup.py` file. You looked into the attributes of the function setup and how these arguments link up to the final installer. Next we added-NumPy related code and added some exception handling code. Finally, we built the installer and learnt how to upload it on the *Cheese Shop* (the PyPI website). In the next chapter, you will be looking at ways to further speed up your Python code by converting parts of it into Cython.

8
Speeding Up NumPy with Cython

Python combined with the NumPy library provides the user with a tool to write highly complex functions and analysis. As the size and complexity of code grow, the number of inefficiencies in the code base starts to creep in. Once the project is in its completion stages, developers should start focusing on the performance of the code and analyze the bottlenecks. Python provides many tools and libraries to create optimized and faster-performing code.

In this chapter, we will be looking at one such tool called Cython. Cython is a static compiler for Python and the language "Cython," which is particularly popular among developers working on scientific libraries/numerical computing. Many famous analytics libraries written in Python make intensive use of Cython (pandas, SciPy, scikit-learn, and so on).

The Cython programming language is a superset of Python and the user still enjoys all the functionalities and higher level constructs provided by Python the language. In this chapter, we will look into a number of reasons why Cython works and you will learn how to convert Python code to Cython. This chapter is not a complete guide to Cython, however.

In this chapter, we will cover the following topics:

- Installing Cython on our computer
- Rewriting a small amount of Python code to the Cython version and analyzing it
- Learning to use NumPy with Cython

The first step toward optimizing code

The questions that every developer should have in mind while optimizing their code are as follows:

- What number of function calls is your code making?
- Are there redundant calls?
- How much memory is the code using?
- Are there memory leaks?
- Where are the bottlenecks?

The first four questions are mostly answered by profiler tools. You are advised to learn at least about one profiling tool. Profiling tools will not be covered in this chapter. In most cases, it is suggested to first try to optimize function calls and memory usage before diving into lower-level approaches such as Cython or assembly languages (in C-derived languages).

Once the bottlenecks have been identified and all the issues with algorithms and logic have been tackled, a Python developer can dive into the world of Cython to get extra speed out of your application.

Setting up Cython

Cython is a compiler that converts Python code with the type definition to C code, which still runs in the Python environment. The final output is native machine code, which runs much faster than the bytecode produced by Python. The magnitude of speed-up for Python code is more evident in code that heavily uses loops. In order to compile C code, the first prerequisite is to have a C/C++ compiler such as `gcc` (Linux) or `mingw` (Windows) installed on the computer.

The second step is to install Cython. Cython comes just like any other library with a Python module and you can install it using any of your preferred methods (pip, easy_install, and so on). Once these two steps are done, you can test your setup by just trying to call Cython from the shell. If you get an error message, then you have missed the second step and you need to reinstall Cython or download the TAR archive from the Cython official website (`http://cython.org/#download`), then run the following command from the `root` folder of this download:

```
python setup.py install
```

Once you have everything done properly, you can proceed to write your first program in Cython.

Hello world in Cython

Cython programs look quite similar to Python ones, mostly with added type information. Let's have a look at a simple program that computes the nth Fibonacci number given n:

```
defcompute_fibonacchi(n):
    """
    Computes fibonacchi sequence

    """

    a = 1
    b = 1
    intermediate = 0
    for x in xrange(n):
intermediate = a
        a = a + b
        b = intermediate
    return a
```

Let's study this program to understand what is going on under the hood when you call this function with some numeric output; let's say `compute_fibonacchi(3)`.

As we know, Python is an interpreted and dynamic language, which means you do not need to declare variables before using them. This means that, at the start of a function call, the Python interpreter is agnostic about the type of value that n will hold. When you call the function with some integral value, Python does the type inference automatically for you by a procedure called **boxing** and **unboxing**.

In Python, everything is an object. So when you type, say, 1 or `hello`, the Python interpreter will internally convert it into objects. This process is also referred to as boxing in a lot of online material. The process could be visualized as:

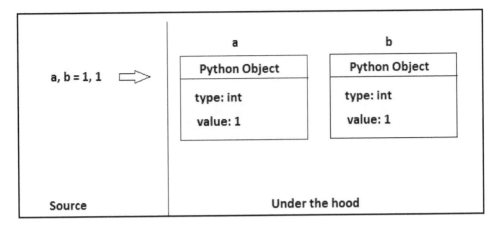

So what happens when you apply functions to objects? The Python interpreter has to do some extra work to infer the type and apply the functions. In a general sense, the following diagram explains the application of the add function in Python. Python being an interpreted language, it does not do a great job in optimizing the function calls, but they can be optimized quite nicely with C or Cython:

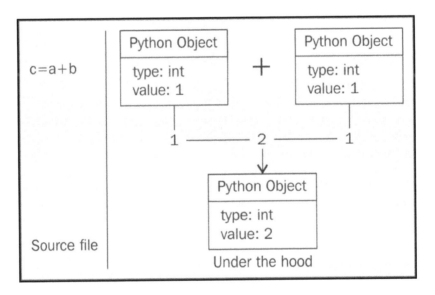

This boxing and unboxing does not come free and takes valuable computing time. The effect becomes more significant when such an operation is performed multiple times in loops.

The following program takes around 1.8 micro seconds per loop on my IPython notebook when run for *n = 20*:

```
In [6]:  timeit(compute_fibonacchi(20))

         100000 loops, best of 3: 1.86 µs per loop
```

Now let's rewrite this program into Cython:

```
defcompute_fibonacchi_cython(int n):
cdefint a, b, intermediate, x
     a, b= 1, 1
     intermediate, x  = 0, 0
     for x in xrange(n):
          intermediate = a
          a = a+b
          b = intermediate
     return a
```

This program takes 64.5 nanoseconds per loop:

```
In [11]:  timeit(compute_fibonacchi_cython(20))

          10000000 loops, best of 3: 64.5 ns per loop
```

Although the speed boost is quite significant in this example code, this is not real-world code that you will encounter, so you should always remember to first run a profiler on the code and identify the sections that require optimization. Also while using Cython, the developer should consider the tradeoff between using static types and flexibility. Using types can cut down flexibility and sometimes readability.

This code could be further improved by removing xrange and using a for loop instead. Once you are satisfied that all the components/functions of the module are properly working and bug-free, the user can store these functions/procedures in a file with a .pyx extension. This is the extension used by Cython. The next step towards integrating this code with your application is to add the information in your setup file.

Here, for illustration purposes, we have stored the code in a file called `fib.pyx` and created a setup file that builds this module:

```
from distutils.core import setup, Extension
from Cython.Build import cythonize
from Cython.Distutils import build_ext

setup(
ext_modules=[Extension('first', ['first.pyx'])],
cmdclass={'build_ext': build_ext}
)
```

Here, note that the name of the extension `first` exactly matches the name of the module. If you fail to maintain the same name, then you will get a cryptic error:

```
C:\dev\packtcode>python setup.py build_ext --inplace
running build_ext
skipping 'first.c' Cython extension (up-to-date)
building 'testing' extension
C:\Anaconda\Scripts\gcc.bat -DMS_WIN64 -mdll -O -Wall -IC:\Anaconda\include -IC:
\Anaconda\PC -c first.c -o build\temp.win-amd64-2.7\Release\first.o
writing build\temp.win-amd64-2.7\Release\testing.def
C:\Anaconda\Scripts\gcc.bat -DMS_WIN64 -shared -s build\temp.win-amd64-2.7\Relea
se\first.o build\temp.win-amd64-2.7\Release\testing.def -LC:\Anaconda\libs -LC:\
Anaconda\PCbuild\amd64 -lpython27 -lmsvcr90 -o C:\dev\packtcode\testing.pyd
Cannot export inittesting: symbol not defined
collect2.exe: error: ld returned 1 exit status
error: command 'C:\\Anaconda\\Scripts\\gcc.bat' failed with exit status 1
```

Multithreaded code

Chances are that your application may be using multithreaded code. Python is not considered suitable for multithreaded code because of the **Global Interpreter Lock** (**GIL**). The good news is that, in Cython, you can explicitly unlock the GIL and make your code truly multithreaded. This is done by simply putting a statement `with nogil:` in your code. You can later acquire the GIL using `with gil` in your code:

```
with nogil:
<The code block here>
function_name(args) with gil:
<function body>
```

NumPy and Cython

Cython has built-in support to provide faster access to NumPy arrays. These facilities make Cython an ideal candidate to optimize NumPy code. For this section, we will study code that calculates the price of the European option, a financial instrument using the Monte-Carlo technique. Knowledge of finance is not expected; however, we assume you have a basic understanding of Monte-Carlo simulations:

```
defprice_european(strike = 100, S0 = 100, time = 1.0,
rate = 0.5, mu = 0.2, steps = 50,
N = 10000, option = "call"):

dt = time / steps
rand = np.random.standard_normal((steps + 1, N))
S = np.zeros((steps+1, N));
S[0] = S0

for t in range(1,steps+1):
S[t] = S[t-1] * np.exp((rate-0.5 * mu ** 2) * dt
+ mu * np.sqrt(dt) * rand[t])
price_call = (np.exp(-rate * time)
* np.sum(np.maximum(S[-1] - strike, 0))/N
price_put = (np.exp(-rate * time)
* np.sum(np.maximum(strike - S[-1], 0))/N

returnprice_call if option.upper() == "CALL" else price_put
```

The following is the Cythonized code for the preceding example:

```
import numpy as np
def price_european_cython(double strike = 100,doubleS0 = 100,
                          double time = 1.0, double rate = 0.5,
                          double mu = 0.2, int steps = 50,
                  long N = 10000, char* option = "call"):
    cdef double dt = time / steps
    cdefnp.ndarray rand = np.random.standard_normal((steps + 1, N))
    cdefnp.ndarray S = np.zeros([steps+1, N], dtype=np.float)
        #cdefnp.ndarrayprice_call = np.zeroes([steps+1,N],
dtype=np.float)
        S[0] = S0

    for t in xrange(1,steps+1):
            S[t] = S[t-1] * np.exp((rate-0.5 * mu ** 2) * dt
                                + mu * np.sqrt(dt) * rand[t])
            price_call = (np.exp(-rate * time)
                    * np.sum(np.maximum(S[-1] - strike, 0))/N
            price_put = (np.exp(-rate * time)
```

```
                        * np.sum(np.maximum(strike - S[-1], 0))/N)

        return price_call if option.upper() == "CALL" else price_put
```

And the setup file for this looks like:

```
from distutils.core import setup, Extension
from Cython.Build import cythonize
from Cython.Distutils import build_ext
import numpy.distutils.misc_util

include_dirs = numpy.distutils.misc_util.get_numpy_include_dirs()


setup(

name="numpy_first",
    version="0.1",
ext_modules=[Extension('dynamic_BS_MC',
                        ['dynamic_BS_MC.pyx'],
include_dirs = include_dirs)],
cmdclass={'build_ext': build_ext}
)
```

While the speed-up gained from Cythonizing the code is great and you may be tempted to write most of the code in Cython, it is recommended to convert only the performance-critical parts to Cython. NumPy has done a great job in optimizing access to arrays and performing faster calculations. This code can be taken as an ideal candidate for depicting the same. The preceding code has a lot of "loose ends" and can be treated as an exercise for you to fix performance issues in Python and using NumPy optimally first before going the Cython way. The speed enhancement from blindly Cythonizing the NumPy code might not be as huge as that for an optimally written code with genuine problems due to the dynamic nature of Python.

To conclude, we present the following that you should follow while developing modules in Cython:

1. Write code in pure Python and test it.
2. Run profilers and identify key areas to focus on.
3. Create a new module to hold Cython code (<module_name>.pyx).
4. Convert all variables and loop indices in these areas to their C counterparts.
5. Test using your previous test setups.
6. Add the extensions into setup files.

Summary

In this chapter, we saw how to covert Python code into Cython. We also looked into some example Python code that involved NumPy arrays. We briefly explained the concept of boxing and unboxing in the Python language and how they affect the performance of code. We also explained how you can explicitly unlock the notorious GIL. To dig further deep in the Cython world, we recommend *Learning Cython Programming, Philip Herron, Packt Publishing*. In the next chapter, you will learn about the NumPy C API and how to use it.

9
Introduction to the NumPy C-API

NumPy is a general-purpose library, designed to address most of the needs of a developer of scientific applications. However, as the code base and coverage of an application increase, so does the computation, and sometimes users demand more specific operations and optimized code segments. We have shown how NumPy and Python have tools, such as f2py and Cython, to address these demands. These tools may be an excellent choice for rewriting your functions to a natively compiled code in order to provide extra speed. But there may be some cases (leveraging a C library, such as **NAG**, to write some analytics) where you may want to do something more radical such as create a new data structure specifically for your own library. This would require you to have access to low-level controls in the Python interpreter. In this chapter, we will be looking into how to do this using the C-API provided by Python and its extension, the NumPy C-API. The C-API itself is a very vast topic and may require a book on its own to fully cover it. Here, we will provide a brief introduction and examples to get you started with the NumPy C-API.

Topics that will be covered in this chapter are:

- The Python C-API and the NumPy C-API
- The basic structure of an extension module
- An introduction to some NumP-specific C-API functions
- Creating functions using the C-API
- Creating a callable module
- Using a module through the Python interpreter and another module

The Python and NumPy C-API

The Python implementation that we are using is a C-based implementation of the Python interpreter. NumPy is specifically for this C-based Python implementation. This implementation of Python comes with a C-API, which is the backbone of the interpreter and provides low-level control to its user. NumPy has further augmented this by providing a rich C-API.

Writing functions in C/C++ can provide developers with the flexibility to leverage some of the advanced libraries available in these languages. However, the cost is apparent in terms of having to write too much boilerplate code around parsing input in order to construct return values. Additionally, developers have to take care while referencing/dereferencing objects since this could eventually create nasty bugs and memory leaks. There is also the problem of future compatibility of the code as the C-API keeps on evolving; hence, if a developer wants to migrate to a later version of Python, they may be up for a lot of maintenance work on these C-API-based extensions. Because of these difficulties, most developers choose to try other optimization techniques. such as Cython or F2PY, before exploring this path. However, there are cases where you would want to reuse some other existing libraries in C/C++, which could suit your specific purpose. In these cases, it might be a good idea to write wrappers over existing functions and expose your Python project.

We will next look at some example code and explain the key functions and macros as we move further along in this chapter. The code given here is compatible with the Python 2.X version and may not work for Python 3.X; however, the process of conversion should be similar.

Developers can try using a tool called **cpychecker** to check for common mistakes while reference counting in a module. Visit `http://gcc-pytho n-plugin.readthedocs.org/en/latest/cpychecker.html` for more details.

The basic structure of an extension module

An extension module written in C will have the following parts:

- A header segment, where you include all your external libraries and `Python.h`
- An initialization segment, where you define the module name and the functions in your C module

- A method structure array to define all the functions in your module
- An implementation segment, where you define all the functions that you would like to expose

The header segment

Header snippets are quite standard, just like a normal C module. We need to include the `Python.h` header file to give our C code access to the internals of the C-API. This file is present in `<path_to_python>/include`. We will be using an array object in our example code, hence we have included the `numpy/arrayobject.h` header file as well. We don't need to specify the full path of the header file here as the path resolution is taken care of in `setup.py`, which we will take a look at later:

```
/*
Header Segment
*/

#include <Python.h>
#include <math.h>
#include <numpy/arrayobject.h>
Initialization Segment
```

The initialization segment

The initialization segment starts with the following:

1. A call to a `PyMODINIT_FUNC` macro. This macro is defined in the Python header and will always be called before you start defining your module.
2. The next line defines the initialization function and is called by the Python interpreter when the function is loaded. The function name has to be in the `init<module_name>` format, the name of the module and functions that your C code is going to expose.

The body of this function contains a call to `Py_InitModule3`, which defines the name of the module and the functions in it. The general structure of this function is as follows:

```
(void)Py_InitModule3(name_of_module, method_array, Docstring)
```

The final call to `import_array()` is a NumPy-specific function, which is required if your functions are using Numpy Array objects. This ensures that the C-API is loaded so that the API table is available if your C++ code uses the C-API. Failure to call this function and use other NumPy API functions will most likely result in a segmentation fault error. You are advised to read about `import_array()` and `import_ufunc()` in the NumPy documentation:

```
/*
Initialization module
*/


PyMODINIT_FUNC
initnumpy_api_demo(void)
{
(void)Py_InitModule3("numpy_api_demo", Api_methods,
        "A demo to show Python and Numpy C-API");
import_array();
}
```

The method structure array

In this segment, you will define the array of methods that your module is going to expose to Python. We have defined two functions here that square its argument. One takes a plain Python double value as input and the second method operates on Numpy Arrays. The `PyMethodDef` structure can be defined in C as follows:

```
Struct PyMethodDef {
char *method_name;
PyCFunction method_function;
int method_flags;
char *method_docstring;
};
```

Here is the description of the members of this structure:

- `method_name`: The name of the function goes here. This will be the name by which the function will be exposed to the Python interpreter.
- `method_function`: This variable holds the name of the C function that is actually called when `method_name` is invoked in the Python interpreter.

- `method_flags`: This tells the interpreter which of the three signatures our function is using. This flag usually has a value of `METH_VARARGS`. This flag can be combined with `METH_KEYWORDS` if you want to allow keyword arguments into your function. This can also have a value of `METH_NOARGS`, which would indicate that you do not want to accept any arguments.
- `method_docstring`: This is the docstring for the function.

This structure needs to be terminated with a sentinel that consists of NULL and 0 as shown in the following example:

```
/*
Method array structure definition
*/
static PyMethodDefApi_methods[] =
{
{"py_square_func", square_func, METH_VARARGS, "evaluate the squares"},
{"np_square", square_nparray_func, METH_VARARGS,  "evaluates the square in
numpy array"},
{NULL, NULL, 0, NULL}
};
```

The implementation segment

The implementation section is the most straightforward section. This is where the C definition of your methods will go. Here, we will study two functions that square their input values. The complexity of these functions is kept low so as to let you focus on the structure of the method.

Creating an array squared function using Python C-API

The Python function passes a reference to itself as the first argument, followed by real arguments given to the function. The `PyArg_ParseTuple` function is used to parse values from the Python function to local variables in the C function. In this function, we cast a value to a double, and hence we use `d` as the second argument. You can see a full list of strings that are accepted by this function at `https://docs.python.org/2/c-api/arg.html`.

The final result of the computations is returned using `Py_Buildvalue`, which takes a similar type of format string to create a Python value from your answer. We use f here, which stands for float, to demonstrate that double and float are treated similarly:

```
/*
Implementation of the actual C funtions
*/

static PyObject* square_func(PyObject* self, PyObject* args)
{
double value;
double answer;

/*  parse the input, from python float to c double */
if (!PyArg_ParseTuple(args, "d", &value))
return NULL;
/* if the above function returns -1, an appropriate Python exception will
* have been set, and the function simply returns NULL
*/

answer = value*value;

return Py_BuildValue("f", answer);
}
```

Creating an array squared function using NumPy C-API

In this section, we will create a function to square all the values of the NumPy Array. The aim here is to demonstrate how to get a NumPy Array in C and then iterate over it. In a real-world scenario, this can be done in an easier way using a map or by vectorizing a square function. We are using the same `PyArg_ParseTuple` function with the `O!` format string. This format string has a `(object)` `[typeobject, PyObject *]` signature and takes the Python type object as the first argument. Users should go through the official API doc to take a look at what other format strings are permissible and which one suits their needs:

 If the passed value does not have the same type, then a `TypeError` is raised.

The following code snippet explain how to parse the argument using `PyArg_ParseTuple`.

```
// Implementation of square of numpy array

static PyObject* square_nparray_func(PyObject* self, PyObject* args)
{

// variable declarations
PyArrayObject *in_array;
PyObject      *out_array;
NpyIter *in_iter;
NpyIter *out_iter;
NpyIter_IterNextFunc *in_iternext;
NpyIter_IterNextFunc *out_iternext;

// Parse the argument tuple by specifying type "object" and putting the
reference in in_array
if (!PyArg_ParseTuple(args, "O!", &PyArray_Type, &in_array))
return NULL;
......
......
```

The next step is to create an array to store its output value and iterators in order to iterate on Numpy Arrays. Note that there is a {handle failure} code at each step when we create an object. This is to ensure that, if anything goes wrong, we can pinpoint the location of the faulty code via debugging:

```
//Construct the output from the new constructed input array
out_array = PyArray_NewLikeArray(in_array, NPY_ANYORDER, NULL, 0);
// Test it and if the input is nothing then just return nothing.
{handle failure}

//  Create the iterators
in_iter = NpyIter_New(in_array, NPY_ITER_READONLY, NPY_KEEPORDER,
NPY_NO_CASTING, NULL);

// {handle failure}

out_iter = NpyIter_New((PyArrayObject *)out_array, NPY_ITER_READWRITE,
NPY_KEEPORDER, NPY_NO_CASTING, NULL);
{handle failure}

in_iternext = NpyIter_GetIterNext(in_iter, NULL);
out_iternext = NpyIter_GetIterNext(out_iter, NULL);
{handle failure}

double ** in_dataptr = (double **) NpyIter_GetDataPtrArray(in_iter);
double ** out_dataptr = (double **) NpyIter_GetDataPtrArray(out_iter);
```

```
A simple handle failure module is like
// {Start handling failure}
if (in_iter == NULL)
// remove the ref and return null
Py_XDECREF(out_array);
return NULL;
// {End handling failure}
```

After taking a look at the preceding boilerplate code, we finally come to the part where all the real action takes place. Those of you who are familiar with C++ will find the method of iteration to be similar to the iteration done over vectors. The `in_iternext` function that we have defined previously comes in handy here and is used to iterate over the Numpy Array. After our while loop, we make sure that we call `NpyIter_Deallocate` on both iterators and `Py_INCREF` on the output array; failing to call these functions is the most common type of mistake that causes memory leaks. Memory leak problems are mostly quite subtle and normally make an appearance when you have a long-running code (such as services or a daemon). To catch these, there is unfortunately no easier way than using a debugger and looking deeper. Sometimes, it helps to just write a couple of `printf` statements, which output the total memory usage:

```
/* iterate over the arrays */
do {
**out_dataptr =pow(**in_dataptr,2);
} while(in_iternext(in_iter) && out_iternext(out_iter));

/* clean up and return the result */
NpyIter_Deallocate(in_iter);
NpyIter_Deallocate(out_iter);
Py_INCREF(out_array);
return out_array;
```

Building and installing the extension module

Once we have written the functions successfully, the next thing to do is build the module and use it in our Python modules. The `setup.py` file looks like the following code snippet:

```
from distutils.core import setup, Extension
import numpy
# define the extension module
demo_module = Extension('numpy_api_demo', sources=['numpy_api.c'],
include_dirs=[numpy.get_include()])

# run the setup
setup(ext_modules=[demo_module])
```

As we are using NumPy-specific headers, we need to have the `numpy.get_include` function in the `include_dirs` variable. To run this setup file, we will use a familiar command:

```
python setup.py build_ext -inplace
```

The preceding command will create a `numpy_api_demo.pyd` file in the directory for us to use in the Python interpreter.

To test our module, we will open a Python interpreter test, and try to call these functions from the module exactly like we do for a module written in Python:

```
>>>import numpy_api_demo as npd
>>> import numpy as np
>>>npd.py_square_func(4)
>>> 16.0
>>> x = np.arange(0,10,1)
>>> y = npd.np_square(x)
```

Summary

In this chapter, we introduced you to yet another way of optimizing or integrating C/C++ code using the C-API provided by Python and NumPy. We explained the basic structure of the code and the additional boilerplate code, which a developer has to write in order to create an extension module. Afterwards, we created two functions that calculated the square of a number and mapped the square function from the `math.h` library to a Numpy Array. The intention here was to familiarize you with how to leverage numerical libraries written in C/C++ to create your own modules with a minimal rewriting of code. The scope for writing C code is much wider than what is described here; however, we hope that this chapter has given you the confidence to leverage the C-API if the need arises.

10
Further Reading

NumPy is a powerful scientific module in Python; hopefully, in the previous nine chapters, we have shown you enough to prove this to you. `ndarray` is the core of all other Python scientific modules. The best way to use NumPy is by using `numpy.ndarray` as the basic data format and combining it with other scientific modules for preprocess, analyze, compute, export, and so on. In this chapter, our focus is on introducing you to a couple of modules that can work with NumPy and make your work/research more efficient.

In this chapter, we will be covering the following topics:

- pandas
- scikit-learn
- netCDF4
- scipy

pandas

pandas is, by far, the most preferable data preprocessing module in Python. The way it handles data is very similar to R. Its data frame not only gives you visually appealing printouts of tables, but also allows you to access data in a more instinctive way. If you are not familiar with R, try to think of using a spreadsheet software such as Microsoft Excel or SQL tables but in a programmatic way. This covers a lot of that what pandas does.

You can download and install pandas from its official site at `http://pandas.pydata.org /`. A more preferable way is to use pip or install Python scientific distributions, such as Anaconda.

Remember how we used `numpy.genfromtxt()` to read the `csv` data in Chapter 4, *NumPy Core and Libs Submodules*? Actually, using pandas to read tables and pass pre-processed data to `ndarray` (simply performing `np.array(data_frame)` will transfer a data frame into a multidimensional `ndarray`) would be a more preferable workflow for analytics. In this section, we are going to show you two basic data structures in pandas: `Series` (for one-dimension) and `DataFrame` (two or multi-dimensions). Then, we will show you how to use pandas to read a table and pass data to

Then, we will show you how to use pandas to read a table and pass data to `ndarray` for further analysis. Let's start with `pandas.Series`:

```
In [1]: import pandas as pd
In [2]: py_list = [3, 8, 15, 25, 11]
In [3]: series = pd.Series(py_list)
In [4]: series
Out[4]:
0     3
1     8
2    15
3    25
4    11
dtype: int64
```

In the preceding example, you can see that we've converted the Python list into a pandas `series` and that, when we printed `series`, the values are lined up perfectly and have an index number associated with them (0 to 4). We can, of course, specify our own index (which starts from *1* or is in the form of alphabets). Take a look at the following code example:

```
In [5]: indices = ['A', 'B', 'C', 'D', 'E']
In [6]: series = pd.Series(py_list, index = indices)
In [7]: series
Out[7]:
A     3
B     8
C    15
D    25
E    11
dtype: int64
```

We changed the indices from numbers to alphabets ranging from *A ~ E*. More conveniently, when we convert a Python dictionary to the pandas `Series`, the key required to do this will become the index automatically. Try practicing converting the dictionary. Next, we are going to explore `DataFrame`, which is the data structure that's used most often in pandas:

```
In [8]: data = {'Name': ['Brian', 'George', 'Kate', 'Amy', 'Joe'],
   ...:          'Age': [23, 41, 26, 19, 35]}
In [9]: data_frame = pd.DataFrame(data)
In [10]: data_frame
Out[10]:
    Age     Name
0   23    Brian
1   41   George
2   26     Kate
3   19      Amy
4   35      Joe
```

In the preceding example, we created `DataFrame`, which contains two columns: the first one is `Name` and the second one is `Age`. You can see from the printouts that it just looks like a table because it's well formatted. Of course, you can also change the index of the data frame. But the advantages of a data frame are much more than just this. We can access or sort the data in each column (by its column name, where two notations are required to access the `data_frame.column_name` or `data_frame[column_name]`); we can even analyze summary statistics. To do this, take a look at this code example:

```
In [11]: data_frame = pd.DataFrame(data)
In [12]: data_frame['Age']
Out[12]:
0    23
1    41
2    26
3    19
4    35
Name: Age, dtype: int64
In [13]: data_frame.sort(columns = 'Age')
Out[13]:
    Age     Name
3   19      Amy
0   23    Brian
2   26     Kate
4   35      Joe
41  George
In [14]: data_frame.describe()
Out[14]:
            Age
count  5.000000
```

```
mean    28.800000
 std     9.011104
 min    19.000000
 25%    23.000000
 50%    26.000000
 75%    35.000000
 max    41.000000
```

In the preceding example, we obtained only the `Age` column and sorted `DataFrame` by `Age`. When we use `describe()`, it calculates summary statistics (including counts, mean, standard deviation, minimum, maximum, and percentiles) for all numeric fields.~~In the last part of this section, we are going to use pandas to read a~~

In the last part of this section, we are going to use pandas to read a `csv` file and pass one field value to `ndarray` for further computation. The `example.csv` file is from the **Office for National Statistics (ONS)**.

Visit `http://www.ons.gov.uk/ons/datasets-and-tables/index.html` for more details. We will use *Sale counts by dwelling type and local authority, England and Wales* on the ONS website. You can search it by the topic name to access the download page or pick any dataset that you are interested in. In the following example, we renamed our example dataset to `sales.csv`:

```
In [15]: sales = pd.read_csv('sales.csv')
In [16]: sales.shape
Out[16]: (348, 97)
In [17]: sales.columns[:3]
Out[17]: Index([u'LA_Code', u'LA_Name', u'1995_COUNT_ALL_TYPES'],
dtype='object')
In [18]: sales['1995_COUNT_ALL_TYPES'].head()
Out[18]:
0    1,188
1    1,652
2    1,684
3    2,314
4    1,558
Name: 1995_COUNT_ALL_TYPES, dtype: object
```

First, we read in `sale.csv` into a `DataFrame` object called `sales`; when we printed out the `shapes` of sales, we found that there were 384 records and 97 columns in the data frame. The return list of the `DataFrame column` attribute is an ordinary Python list, and we printed out the first three columns in the data: `LA_Code`, `LA_Name`, and `1995_COUNT_ALL_TYPES`. Then, we printed the first five records in `1995_COUNT_ALL_TYPES` using the `head()` function (the `tail()` function will print the last five records).

Again, pandas is a powerful preprocessing module in Python (its data handling in general more than its preprocessing power, but in the preceding example, we only covered the preprocessing part), and it has many handy functions to help you clean your data and prepare your analytics. This section is just an introduction; there is a lot that we can't cover due to space restrictions, such as pivoting, `datetime`, and more. Hopefully, you can get the idea and start making your scripts more efficient.

scikit-learn

Scikit is short for SciPy Toolkits, which are add-on packages for SciPy. It provides a wide range of analytics modules and scikit-learn is one of them; this is by far the most comprehensive machine learning module for Python. scikit-learn provides a simple and efficient way to perform data mining and data analysis, and it has a very active user community.

You can download and install scikit-learn from its official website at `http://scikit-learn.org/stable/`. If you are using a Python scientific distribution, such as Anaconda, it is included here as well.

Now, it's time for some machine learning using scikit-learn. One of the advantages of scikit-learn is that it provides some sample datasets (demo datasets) for practice. Let's load the diabetes dataset first.

```
In [1]: from sklearn.datasets import load_diabetes
In [2]: diabetes = load_diabetes()
In [3]: diabetes.data
Out[3]:
array([[ 0.03807591,  0.05068012,  0.06169621, ..., -0.00259226,
         0.01990842, -0.01764613],
       [-0.00188202, -0.04464164, -0.05147406, ..., -0.03949338,
        -0.06832974, -0.09220405],
       [ 0.08529891,  0.05068012,  0.04445121, ..., -0.00259226,
         0.00286377, -0.02593034],
       ...,
       [ 0.04170844,  0.05068012, -0.01590626, ..., -0.01107952,
        -0.04687948,  0.01549073],
       [-0.04547248, -0.04464164,  0.03906215, ...,  0.02655962,
         0.04452837, -0.02593034],
       [-0.04547248, -0.04464164, -0.0730303 , ..., -0.03949338,
        -0.00421986,  0.00306441]])
In [4]: diabetes.data.shape
Out[4]: (442, 10)
```

We loaded a sample dataset called `diabetes` from `sklearn.datasets`; it contains 442 observations, 10 dimensions, and ranges from -2 to 2. The `Toy` dataset also provides labeled data for supervised learning (if you are not familiar with machine learning, try to think of the labelled data as categories). In our example, labeled data from the `diabetes` dataset can be called from `diabetes.target`, and it has a range from 25 to 346.

Remember how we performed linear regression in Chapter 5, *Linear Algebra in Numpy*? We're going to perform it one more time using scikit-learn instead. Again, I recommend that, when you're developing a script to help you in your research or analytics, use NumPy `ndarray` as your general data format; however, for computation, using scipy, scikit-learn, or other scientific modules would be more preferable. One advantage of machine learning is model evaluation (where you train and test the result). Using this, we will split our data into two datasets: training datasets and test datasets, and then pass the two datasets for the purpose of linear regression:

```
In [5]: from sklearn.cross_validation import train_test_split
In [6]: X_train, X_test, y_train, y_test  =
        train_test_split(diabetes.data,
diabetes.target,
random_state = 50)
```

In the preceding example, we split up the diabetes dataset into training and test datasets (for both the data and its categories) using the `train_test_split()` function. The first two parameters are arrays that we want to split; the `random_state` parameter is optional, which means that a pseudo random number generator state is used for random sampling. The default split ratio is 0.25, which means that 75% of the data is split into the training set and 25% is split into the test set. You can try to print out the training/test datasets we just created to take a look at its distribution (in the preceding code example, `X_train` represents the training dataset for the diabetes data, `X_test` represents the diabetes test data, `y_train` represents the categorized diabetes training data, and `y_test` represents the categorized diabetes test data).

Next, we are going to fit our datasets into a linear regression model:

```
In [7]: from sklearn.linear_model import LinearRegression
In [8]: lr = LinearRegression()
In [9]: lr.fit(X_train, y_train)
Out[9]: LinearRegression(copy_X = True, fit_intercept = True,
     Normalize = False)
In [10]: lr.coef_
Out[10]:
array([  80.73490856, -195.84197988,  474.68083473,  371.06688824,
        -952.26675602,  611.63783483,  174.40777144,  159.78382579,
         832.01569658,   12.04749505])
```

First, we created a `LinearRegression` object from `sklearn.linear_model` and used the `fit()` function to fit the `X_train` and `y_train` datasets. We can check the estimated coefficients for the linear regression by calling its `coef_` attribute. Furthermore, we can use the fitted linear regression for prediction. Take a look at the following example:

```
In [11]: lr.predict(X_test)[:10]
Out[11]:
array([  71.96974998,    82.55916305,   265.71560021,    79.37396336,
         72.48674613,    47.01580194,   149.11263906,   185.36563936,
         94.88688296,   132.08984366])
```

The `predict()` function is used to predict the test dataset based on the linear regression we fit with the training datasets; in the preceding example, we printed out the first 10 predicted values. Here is the plot of the predicted and test value of y:

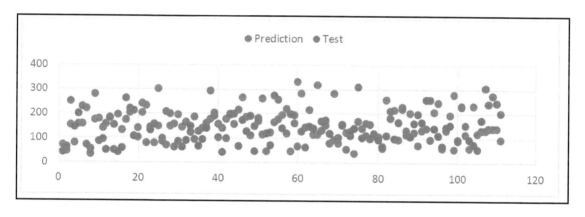

```
In [12]: lr.score(X_test, y_test)
Out[12]: 0.48699089712593369
```

Then, we can check the determination R-square of the prediction using the `score()` function.

This is pretty much the standard fitting and predicting process in scikit-learn, and it's pretty intuitive and easy to use. Of course, besides regression, there are many analytics that scikit-learn can carry out such as classification, clustering, and modeling. Hope this section helps you in your scripts.

netCDF4

netCDF4 is the fourth version of the netCDF library that's implemented on top of HDF5 (Hierarchical Data Format, designed to store and organize large amounts of data), which makes it possible to manage extremely large and complex multidimensional data. The greatest advantage of netCDF4 is that it is a completely portable file format with no limit on the number or size of data objects in a collection, and it's appendable while being archivable as well. Many scientific research organizations use it for data storage. Python also has an interface to access and create this type of data format.

You can download and install the module from its official documentation page at `http://unidata.github.io/netcdf4-python/`, or clone it from its GitHub repository at `https://github.com/Unidata/netcdf4-python`. It's not included in the standard Python Scientific distribution, but it's built into NumPy and can build with Cython (this is recommended but not required).

For the following example, we are going to use the sample `netCDF4` file on the Unidata website at `http://www.unidata.ucar.edu/software/netcdf/examples/files.html`, and we will use the climate system model as an example: `sresa1b_ncar_ccsm3-example.nc`

First, we will use the `netCDF4` module to explore the dataset a bit, and extract the values we need for further analysis:

```
In [1]: import netCDF4 as nc
In [2]: dataset = nc.Dataset('sresa1b_ncar_ccsm3-example.nc', 'r')
In [3]: variables = [var for var in dataset.variables]
In [4]: variables
Out[4]:
['area', 'lat', 'lat_bnds', 'lon', 'lon_bnds', 'msk_rgn', 'plev',
'pr', 'tas', 'time', 'time_bnds', 'ua']
```

We imported the python `netCDF4` module, and we used the `Dataset()` function to read the sample `netCDF4` file. The `r` parameter means the file is in read-only mode, so we can also specify `a` when we want to append the file or `w` to create a new file. Then, we obtained all the variables stored in the dataset and saved them to a list called variables (note that the variables attribute will return a Python dictionary of the object of the variables). Lastly, we printed out the variables in the dataset using this command:

```
In [5]: precipitation = dataset.variables['pr']
In [6]: precipitation.standard_name
Out[6]: 'precipitation_flux'
In [7]: precipitation.missing_value
Out[7]: 1e+20
```

```
In [8]: precipitation.ndim
Out[8]: 3
In [9]: precipitation.shape
Out[9]: (1, 128, 256)
In [10]: precipitation[:, 1, :10]
Out[10]:
array([[ 8.50919207e-07,    8.01471970e-07,    7.74396426e-07,
         7.74230614e-07,    7.47181844e-07,    7.21426375e-07,
         7.19294349e-07,    6.99790974e-07,    6.83397502e-07,
         6.74683179e-07]], dtype=float32)
```

In the preceding example, we picked a variable named `pr` and saved it to `precipitation`. As we all know `netCDF4` is a self-describing file format; you can create and access any user-defined attribute stored in the variable, though the most common one is `standard_name`, which tells us that the variable represents the precipitation flux. We checked another commonly used attribute, `missing_value`, which represents the no-data value stored in the `netCDF4` file. Then, we printed the number of dimensions of the precipitation variable by its `ndim` and the shape by the `shape` attribute. Lastly, we want to get the value of row 1, that is, the first 10 columns in the `netCDF4` file; to do this, just use the indexing as we always do.

Next, we are going to cover the basics of creating a `netCDF4` file and storing a three-dimensional NumPy `ndarray` as a variable:

```
In [11]: import numpy as np
In [12]: time = np.arange(10)
In [13]: lat = 54 + np.random.randn(8)
In [14]: lon = np.random.randn(6)
In [15]: data = np.random.randn(480).reshape(10, 8, 6)
```

First, we prepared a three-dimensional `ndarray` (data) to store in the `netCDF4` file; the data is built in three dimensions, which are time (`time`, size of 10), latitude (`lat`, size of 8), and longitude (`lon`, size of 6). In `netCDF4`, time is not a `datetime` object, but the number of time units (these can be seconds, hours, days, and so on) from the defined start time (specified in the `unit` attribute; we will explain this to you later). Now, we have all the data we want to store in the file, so let's build the netCDF structure:

```
In [16]: output = nc.Dataset('test_output.nc', 'w')
In [17]: output.createDimension('time', 10)
In [18]: output.createDimension('lat', 8)
In [19]: output.createDimension('lon', 6)
In [20]: time_var = output.createVariable('time', 'f4', ('time',))
In [21]: time_var[:] = time
In [22]: lat_var = output.createVariable('lat', 'f4', ('lat',))
In [23]: lat_var[:] = lat
```

```
In [24]: lon_var = output.createVariable('lon', 'f4', ('lon',))
In [25]: lon_var[:] = lon
```

We initialized the netCDF4 file by specifying the file path and using the w write mode. Then, we built the structure using createDimension() to specify the dimensions: time, lat, and lon. Each dimension has a variable to represent its values, just like the scales for an axis. Next, we are going to save the three-dimensional data to the file:

```
In [26]: var = output.createVariable('test', 'f8', ('time', 'lat', 'lon'))
In [27]: var[:] = data
```

The creation of a variable always starts with the createVariable() function and specifies the variable name, variable datatype, and the dimensions associated with it. The second step is to pass the same shape of ndarray into the declared variable. Now that we have the entire data store in the file, we can specify the attribute to help describe the dataset. The following example uses the time variable to show how we can specify the attribute:

```
In [28]: time_var.standard_name = 'Time'
In [29]: time_var.units = 'days since 2015-01-01 00:00:00'
In [30]: time_var.calendar = 'gregorian'
```

So, now that the time variable has the unit and calendar associated with it, the ndarray time will be converted to a date based on the unit and calendar that we specified; this is similar to all the variables. When the creation of netCDF4 file is done, the last step is to close the file connection:

```
In [31]: output.close()
```

The preceding code shows you the usage of Python netCDF4 API in order to read and create a netCDF4 file. This module doesn't include any scientific computations (so it's not included in any Python scientific distribution), but the target is in the interface for the file I/O, which can be the very first or last stage in your research and analytics.

SciPy

SciPy is a well-known Python library focusing on scientific computing (it contains modules for optimization, linear algebra, integration, interpolation, and special functions such as FFT, signal, and image processing). It builds on the NumPy Array object, and NumPy is part of the whole SciPy stack (remember that we introduced the Scientific Python family in Chapter 1, *An Introduction to NumPy*). However, the SciPy module contains various topics that we can't cover in just one section. Let's look at an example of image processing (noise removal) to help you get some idea of what SciPy can do:

```
In [1]: from scipy.misc import imread, imsave, ascent
In [2]: import matplotlib.pyplot as plt
In [3]: image_data = ascent()
```

First, we import three functions from SciPy's miscellaneous routines: `imread`, `imsave`, and `ascent`. In the following example, we use the built-in image `ascent`, which is a 512 by 512 greyscale image. Of course, you may use your own image; simply call `imread('your_image_name')` and it will load as an `ndarray`.

The `pyplot` result from the `matplotlib` module we imported here is just for displaying the image; we did this in Chapter 6, *Fourier Analysis in NumPy*. Here is the built-in image `ascent`:

Now, we can add some noise to the image and use the `pyplot` module to show the noised image:

```
In [4]: import numpy as np
In [5]:noise_img = image_data +  image_data.std() *
np.random.random(image_data.shape)
In [6]: imsave('noise_img.png', noise_img)
In [7]: plt.imshow(noise_img)
```

```
Out[7]: <matplotlib.image.AxesImage at 0x20066572898>
In [8]: plt.show()
```

In this code snippet, we import `numpy` to generate some random noise based on the image shape. Then, we save the noised image to `noise_img.png`. The noised image looks like this:

Next, we are going to use the multidimensional image-processing module in SciPy, `scipy.ndimage`, to apply filters to the noised image in order to smooth it. The `ndimage` module provides various filters; for a detailed list, refer to `http://docs.scipy.org/doc/scipy/reference/ndimage.html`, but in the following example, we will just use the Gaussian and Uniform filters:

```
In [9]: from scipy import ndimage
In [10]: gaussian_denoised = ndimage.gaussian_filter(noise_img, 3)
In [11]: imsave('gaussian_denoised.png', gaussian_denoised )
In [12]: plt.imshow(gaussian_denoised)
Out[12]: <matplotlib.image.AxesImage at 0x2006ba54860>
In [13]: plt.show()
```

```
In [14]: uniform_denoised = ndimage.uniform_filter(noise_img)
In [15]: imsave('uniform_denoised.png', uniform_denoised)
In [16]: plt.imshow(gaussian_denoised)
Out[17]: <matplotlib.image.AxesImage at 0x2006ba80320>
In [18]: plt.show()
```

First, we import `ndimage` from SciPy, apply the Gaussian filter on `noise_image`, set the `sigma` (the standard deviation for the Gaussian kernel) to 3, and save it to `gaussian_denoised.png`. Look at the the left-hand side of the preceding image. In general, the larger the sigma, the smoother the image will be, which means a loss of detail. The second filter we applied is the Uniform filter and took all the default values for the parameters, which results in the right-hand part of the previous image. Though the uniform filter retains more details from the raw image, the image still contains noise.

The previous example was a simple image-processing example using SciPy. However, SciPy can do more than image processing, it can also perform many types of analytical/scientific computation. For details, refer to *Learning SciPy for Numerical and Scientific Computing, Second Edition, Packt Publishing*.

Summary

NumPy is certainly the core to scientific computation using Python: many modules are based on it. Although sometimes you might find that NumPy has no analytics modules, it certainly provides you with a way of reaching out to a wide range of scientific modules.

We hope the last chapter of this book has given you a good idea about using these modules with NumPy and makes your script more efficient (there are still so many handy NumPy modules we can't cover in this book; just spend an afternoon on GitHub or PyPI, and you may find a handful of them). Last but not least, thank you for spending time with us going through so many functions. Have some fun with NumPy now!

Index